Breaking Through

Lives Changed in the Heart of the City

Breaking Through

Lives Changed in the Heart of the City

Roger Huang

with

Susanna Foth Aughtmon

Bold Vision Books
PO Box 2011
Friendswood, Texas 77549

Breaking Through

has not been written to boast of what we do and who we are
but to remember His love for a desolate community.

A few people wonder why I wrote a second book.
It is simply because
I don't ever want to forget
God's faithfulness, kindness, and generosity
to a group of lost souls.

Table of Contents

Foreword by Michelle Huang ~9

Introduction: A New Challenge ~11

Chapter 1: Life in the Tenderloin ~17

    George's Story

Chapter 2: Hearts Thrown Wide Open ~24

    A City Academy Story

Chapter 3: A Life Turned Inside Out ~30

    An SFCA Summer Camp Story

Chapter 4: Coordinating Passions ~37

    A Praise Report from a City Impact Volunteer

Chapter 5: A Joyful Life ~46

    A Faith Story from a Tenderloin Resident

Chapter 6: A Firm Foundation ~55

    A Thank You Letter from a Tenderloin Resident

    A Rescue Mission Story

Chapter 7: Healing Bodies, Healing Hearts ~67

    A Letter of Hope

Chapter 8: A Turk Street Breakthrough ~81

    A Letter of Appreciation from a Tenderloin Resident

Chapter 9: A Trust Adventure ~89

    Pushpa's Story

Chapter 10: A Building Miracle ~99

    Rebecca's Story

Chapter 11: The Taylor Street Breakthrough ~106

A Letter of Gratitude

Chapter 12: A Beautiful Journey ~115

Terry's Story

An Internship Story

A Rescue Mission Breakthrough

Chapter 13: Super Saturdays Are Super Again ~127

A Super Saturday Update

Chapter 14: Love Comes Full Circle ~134

Conclusion: A New Path ~139

Thoughts on Breakthroughs ~144

Afterword by Christian Huang ~148

About the Authors ~150

Acknowledgments ~152

City Impact Information ~154

~

Foreword

There will never be another man so pure in his intentions, so obvious with his gestures, or so misunderstood by his words. My dad, Roger, is unpolished in his agenda yet so influential with his life. Ever since I can remember, I have always known who he was and continues to be. Nothing can deter me from believing that his heart is pure and worth defending. I watched him being the best person he could be while simultaneously overcoming a scarred past. He gives the best of himself to others. He makes it his mission to protect the community before the ministry of San Francisco City Impact, the family, and the relationships he values.

Breaking Through is a compilation of stories of those who are doing their best to explore their full potential. They are making tangible, life-altering decisions to impact the world around them. Roger has touched everyone that crosses his path. The reason I know this is because the way he lived impacted me. When he spent time with a lonely kid, the poor, a wealthy donor looking for purpose, a struggling young couple exploring how to coexist and find purpose, or individuals looking for direction, he took time away from his family to do that. He took time away from me. He knew that my mom was doing a good job handling everything at home, allowing him the freedom to spend time with others. He has always poured out his life in service.

The heart of this man is showing people how to break through the mundane. It is how my dad spends his life. He maximizes every opportunity and diversifies every resource to ensure that his time is well spent protecting the community. He wants to be sure the lonely are reached. He is not moved by networkers, big names, and those that just want to make a name for themselves. What you see is what you get with him. Life in ministry is not as glamorous as people think it is. But it's real. And it makes a difference.

As his daughter who has grown up in this work, I have seen Roger stay true to his passion for helping the poor. I've seen many lives changed, and I have been a part of some of those changes. I have learned a lot along the way. I learned you have to be raw and compassionate. There are sacrifices that must be made for breakthroughs to happen. But as long as you persevere, you'll learn how to navigate your own life by following God's lead. This is what makes an impact. If you are compassionate with the person next to you, then God can use you. The difference you make in yourself and others will slowly evolve. You will see how God can work through you. Breakthroughs are not just for me or my dad. You, too, can make a difference.

I hope you are inspired as you read these breakthrough stories. One person can touch many. You can be that person!

~Michelle Huang

~

Introduction

A New Challenge

The San Francisco Tenderloin is not the place where most people choose to spend their lives. As I walk to our Jones Street building, I smell the same smells that I smelled thirty years ago when I walked up this street. The smoky exhaust of the cars crawling through the intersection. The sharp smell of tar as I pass a street construction crew. A hint of old garbage lurking in the entrance to an open alleyway. Some of the sights are the same, too. Buildings need repair. Police cars patrol the area.

But I don't come to the Tenderloin for the smells or sights. I come for the people. The tired and worn out. The brokenhearted. The elderly that push their handcarts to the corner market. The loud kids that break into a run at the sight of Boeddeker Park. The homeless contingent that wraps themselves up in old sleeping bags on cold nights. The immigrant families that crowd twelve people into a studio apartment. These are the people I come for. They pull me here with their needs and their fears and their hopes.

Although some may not know where to look, there is beauty and joy in this corner of San Francisco. It is found in seeing people come to know Jesus and seeing their lives change. Although the smells haven't changed in this cramped district, I have been here long enough to see people become more than they ever dreamed they could be. Their lives were changed forever. One of those lives was mine. That keeps me coming back. Day after day. Week after week. Year after year.

As I push open the door of San Francisco City Academy, I hear the laughter of kids down the hall. Those kids are the bright hope of the Tenderloin. Kids who are being given a chance at joy and growth. Kids who are learning to add and subtract, to read with confidence, and to know the love of Jesus. They know they have a place to come and an amazing group of teachers and volunteers to serve them. This is one of the most beautiful gifts God ever gave us. He created a haven of safety and love for children in one of the most broken areas of the city. When we opened City Academy with six children fifteen years ago, we never guessed that attendance would someday be nearly a hundred students. Soon their numbers will push us out of the building. That is the plan. When this miracle building was renovated, we hoped to see 300 students fill up every nook and cranny of its space. We are well on our way.

I open the door to the back staircase and head up to the third floor to my office. I have a full day planned, and I want to get started. I am not big on sitting around. I don't spend a lot of time in my office. I don't travel a lot, or speak at conferences. I want to be out in the community. I want to be here with the poor and broken. That is what keeps me grounded and fires me up at the same time. There is so much to do. But I have learned that God is the One who does the miracles in His timing and in His way. I am just His bellhop. I get to open doors, and He does all the work.

Chasing God in the Tenderloin isn't something I planned on doing. But God planned it for me. Growing up in an abusive home in Taiwan, I had a hard time believing that I had a future. When my family immigrated to San Francisco in the 1970s, I found my way out. I left home at seventeen. Escaping the stinging blows of my father and the neglect of my mother, I never looked back. I slept in doorways and in hotel lobbies. Anything was better than staying home. I chased after success, working my way up the ladder in the hotel industry. I thought money would bring stability. I often held two jobs at a time, trying to gain that sense of security that I longed for. Chasing success didn't offer me much in the way of peace. My brokenness, my deep need for love, and my inability to connect with others kept me in a place of pain. Even after I met the love of my life, Maite, a beautiful Basque girl with a smile that lit up my world, I couldn't fill that huge hole in my soul. I needed more love than any one person could offer me. Then Maite found God. And God found me. He chased me down with His love, and I have been chasing Him back ever since.

12

He led me here. I was a new believer and an auditor at a new five-star hotel. I had a loving wife and four beautiful kids. I thought I was doing pretty well. God thought I could do better. When my car broke down in the Tenderloin, my first thought was, "Get out as fast as you can."

His thought was, "Let's see how long we can get you to stay." As I waited for a tow truck, I saw a young boy get beat up on the corner. I couldn't stand the violence of it. It reminded me of my own painful experiences as a child. I drove away, thinking of myself and my family and that all I wanted was to go home.

On the way home, God spoke to me for the first time. The thought that came to me was this: "What would you have done if that was your son?" I knew it was the Holy Spirit.

I answered, "I would have protected him."

The Spirit's reply was, "They are all the same to me." I knew in that moment that I had turned my back on one of His kids and that I had broken His heart.

From that point on, my life was changed. God broke my heart for the Tenderloin. I knew that if I was going to chase God, this was the place where He was leading me. He wanted me to see myself in the faces of the broken. To recognize that any one of the people on these dirty streets could be my aunt or uncle, my son or daughter. He wanted me to identify with their pain and show them the way to hope. He wanted me to know that He loved every single person crammed into this fifty-block radius; and if I was going to love Him, loving them was part of the bargain. He didn't have to ask me twice. I showed up the next day with a bag full of sandwiches to hand out to the hungry. I have been showing up every day since.

Maite and I could never have known what would happen after giving away that bag of bologna sandwiches. Our journey has been a roller-coaster ride of highs and lows, of deep disappointments and miracles so great that we still have trouble wrapping our minds around them. We have grown from a mom-and-pop team to a multi-site ministry that reaches our community through a rescue mission, thrift shop, elementary and middle school, free medical clinic, food bank, community church, and more.

We host thousands of volunteers that pour into the Tenderloin each year to minister by serving meals, delivering groceries, and praying. We went from earning a stable salary in secular jobs to relying on God's provision through prayer and fasting. We fasted for everything. For favor, for paychecks, for food, for buildings, for revival, for breakthroughs, for miracles. And God came through over and over. He is still coming through. Every Wednesday our entire staff sets aside the day for prayer. It is the only way that we know how to live. It is the only thing that makes a difference. We pray and believe that God will do what we cannot. And He always does. In His time. In His way.

As I walk down the third-floor hall to my office, I have to smile. The laughter coming from the offices at the other end is contagious. The development team is at work. I'm sure my daughter, Michelle, is in the middle of it. I am continuously amazed by the woman she has become. She does a hundred big and small tasks that make the ministry run smoothly. Opening the door to my office, I step inside and get a pot of coffee going. If I am in the building, you will find me here. It's a calm place in a ministry center that doesn't have a whole lot of quiet. If there is a deep need that Maite and I are praying for, I go away, out to the Blessing House in Fort Bragg to pray.

God has proven time and time again, if we wait on Him and listen for Him, He shows up. We have done a lot of waiting over the years. In the last few years, the prayers I have been praying have been different. The desperate prayers of a new ministry have given way to the prayers of a growing, changing ministry. One of the biggest changes for me is that I am no longer in charge.

Two years ago, I stepped down from official leadership of City Impact and into an advisory role as my son, Christian, took over the role of Executive Director. We have come a long way from feeding the homeless with a pot of steamed rice in the back room of a rented building. Christian has the vision and stamina to carry the ministry forward. Maite and I have never been more proud of him. But I would be lying if I said the change has been an easy adjustment. No change ever is. It has been a shift for me to yield the shouldering of the ministry to someone else. It has been a release, but it has been hard to let go.

I have had to find a new path and a new way to live out the vision that God planted in my heart. I still meet with the incoming teams and with our donors. I still love talking to the kids from City Academy. I serve at the Rescue Mission and meet with pastors. But the thing that has amazed me is the stream of workers that God is sending to take up the work of loving the poor here. For years, Maite and I prayed for God to send people to work with us. At first, we just had our kids. Then, slowly, one by one, more people began to come. Each of their journeys is unique. When I see the way God has worked to bring each of our staff members, our donors, our volunteers, and those we minister to through our doors, I am blown away by His creativity.

With a hot cup of coffee in hand, I can't help thinking that the people God has brought are a testament to His faithfulness. Working in the Tenderloin will never be easy. There is no quick fix to transforming people's lives. People who come here looking for immediate results go away disappointed. But I have found that the longer we stay, the more we get to see God work. There is a certain amount of stubbornness required for working in this part of the city. We don't see big numbers and mass conversions; but with longevity, we can make a difference in the community.

Those of us who stay don't try out new ministry techniques each week or sing the latest worship songs. We don't know exactly what God is doing when we get here, but we pray, we love, we serve daily—and we stay. It's like a marriage. We are in it for the good times and the bad. We are completely committed. I see this commitment in the people that I rub shoulders with every day. I see their humility and their compassion. Their purpose in life is to make a difference. I see them pour themselves out, day after day, and it inspires me.

We are compelled by the hurting, not by the excitement of an event or program. Working with the needy is not a feel-good job. It is completely overwhelming and impossible. But we serve a God who likes the impossible. If we are willing to serve alongside Him, God will let us in on what He is doing. I have said it a million times: He is the One who is doing the great work in the Tenderloin. God is gracious enough to let us be a part of it. When I see people coming to City Impact, moved by compassion for the wounded, I see the heart of God. The heart of the One who loves and transforms.

The stories of those whose lives were changed in the Tenderloin are too many to recount. But I want to share some stories that have touched my heart, encouraged me, and brought me hope. These are stories of courage and commitment. They are love stories. These are people that I love, and people who have offered up their lives to the God who never stops chasing us. He is close to the brokenhearted, and He wants us right there with Him. These are the stories of the ones who have thrown off everything to come and serve, the ones who show up in the Tenderloin even when their own hearts are broken.

God is not only interested in transforming the lives of the needy. He is also working in the lives of those who come to bring about change. That means change begins in their own hearts, with their own desires and hopes and dreams. He is breaking through, filling them up, and reshaping their lives. One person at a time.

~

Chapter 1

Life in the Tenderloin

I rarely sit at my computer. I like to visit the different parts of the ministry and connect with the staff who are so hard at work. I am amazed and humbled to see people putting their hearts and souls into this work. Answering one last e-mail, I log off my computer and head out the door to see what is up for San Francisco City Impact today. There is always some kind of craziness going on. It wouldn't be the Tenderloin if there wasn't. Maite and I just laugh. God has called us to a crazy life. The best part is seeing how He comes up with crazy solutions to our crazy problems. He always has better ideas and better plans than we could ever imagine.

Walking by our commercial kitchen, I hear a hum of activity. The newly renovated kitchen works like a restaurant kitchen for serving healthy meals to the City Academy students every day. For some of our students, lunch is their best meal of the day. We want to nurture their minds and the bodies. It's hard to learn on an empty stomach. With all the food donations we get from the surrounding grocery stores and commercial kitchens, the kids get a healthy variety. Recently, someone donated hundreds of gourmet pre-made meals. Those meals put our old peanut butter-and-jelly sandwiches that we used to make to shame. We are always amazed by the food that comes in and God's timing in His provision. Just a few weeks ago, we planned a movie night for our friends at the Rescue Mission and bags of pre-popped popcorn showed up in the donations that day. We couldn't help laughing. You can't watch a movie without popcorn. God surprised us once more with His goodness.

Looking into the kitchen, I see Veasna hard at work with his ministry students from our School of Ministry. Veasna is at the stove. The ministry students are chopping vegetables and getting ready for the lunch hour. Each School of Ministry student spends time every day learning about God and serving others in one of our City Impact ministries. One of the ministry students once asked Veasna, "Who is your favorite ministry student?"

He said, "Whoever is here working in the kitchen." Veasna always gives the best answers. Each morning, the kitchen crew determines what the meal will be—based on what food has come in. They have to be creative and fast. From the smell of the onions sautéing in the pan, I would say it is going to be a great lunch. Veasna is a hard worker and always does his best in whatever area he is asked to serve.

Veasna is a like a son to me. He has been with City Impact for the last sixteen years, but he has lived in the Tenderloin as long as he can remember. His story is like so many of those who have come here as immigrants. He has known pain and suffering. His parents escaped the killing fields of Cambodia and the brutal regime of the Khmer Rouge. They made a midnight escape through the jungles to a refugee camp when Veasna's mother was pregnant with him. Surviving snipers and land mines, they made it to the camp only to watch people die of starvation. It seemed like there was no hope, and they were the lucky ones. Behind them, lay the destruction of their home and country. They managed to get out with their lives. Veasna's family wanted a new start. They arrived in San Francisco, only to find another kind of brutality—life in the Tenderloin.

Life in the Tenderloin can feel hopeless. Poverty is the norm. Children are exposed to drugs, gangs, and the sex industry on a daily basis. It is not unusual to see more than one drug dealer and several porn shops on one city block. Families have to scrimp just to make ends meet and often don't have enough money for life's basics. For those coming from overseas, language barriers and culture shock can be overwhelming. Veasna's family, like most, was unprepared. This was not the American dream. It was more of an American nightmare.

After years of struggle, Veasna's family began to fall apart. His father, an educated scholar, left the family in the Tenderloin to find work back in Cambodia. Many of his family members turned to drugs and gangs simply to survive on the streets. You do what you have to do to put food on the table. While some immigrant children can find a way to fit in to their new environment in school, Veasna could not connect. Schoolwork was difficult. He couldn't sit

18

still or concentrate. He acted out in class. Teachers were thankful to move him on to the next grade. Veasna, like so many other kids who struggle with learning, fell through the cracks. He fell in with many of his family members, selling drugs, becoming a gangster, and escaping the pain of his life through the drug Ecstasy.

The sound of laughter cuts through my thoughts.

"Okay, let's hurry it up," Veasna says as he moves from one station to the next, directing his ministry students as they finish prep before lunch. Hungry schoolkids wait for no one.

Most people who grow up in the Tenderloin want to get out. They want to do more than just survive. But for those stuck in the cycle of poverty and suffering on a daily basis, alcohol and drugs are an immediate way to escape. Those who use drugs are here in body, but not in spirit. Veasna bought into that lie. When he was drunk or high, he didn't feel his suffering. If he could just make it to the next party or the next weekend, he could keep living. He wanted to offer the same escape to his friends and family. Unfortunately, drugs are a temporary fix to a permanent problem. The high never lasts. And the sense of loneliness and despair comes crashing back as soon as the drugs wear off.

It is easy to forget his story as I watch him now. Veasna is a solid leader. No matter where we ask Veasna to serve, he is willing. For years, he worked at City Academy, teaching physical education. When we asked him to be in charge of the commercial kitchen, he didn't blink. It shows how much his heart has changed over the course of the years. The drug dealing gangster with a reputation as fierce as the pit bulls he used to raise is now a Christ follower. His life looks nothing like it did. He is a caring husband, married to Elaine, one of our schoolteachers, who gave up her career in the secular world to come teach at City Academy. And the boy whose father walked away has become a man who can't stop grinning when he talks about his own kids. Their entire family is a part of who we are as a ministry.

Sixteen years ago, Veasna found a different kind of high. He had been to City Impact outreaches as a kid, but the truth of who Jesus was and His love hadn't sunk in. It is hard to have hope when you are struggling to survive. But one morning he was sleeping off a high in one of our church services and Veasna felt the power of the Holy Spirit for the first time. It was like no feeling he had ever experienced. No high could compare to the grace and peace he felt flood his body. It began to change his heart. He wanted more of that feeling. The tough Cambodian gangster yielded his life to God. What else could he do? Since that day, he has never been the same.

His life has not been perfect or without struggles. Throwing off an old way of life never is. But since that morning, he has become a part of us. As he asked Jesus to be a part of those struggles, he began to become more and more like Him. With each day, he has faced his fears. He has stepped out of the life he knew and embraced the new life that God offered him—a life that invites him to be more and do more than he ever thought he could. A few years ago, I told him I wanted him to get his pastor's license. He looked at me like I had lost my mind. But Veasna has a pastors' heart for this community. His life is tethered to these streets and these people. He ministers daily to the ministry students and City Academy students. He got that license.

Veasna is on a mission to see his family and friends come to know the same grace and peace he found in Jesus. We have watched him grow and change in these last sixteen years. He is not the same man he once was. It is beautiful to see him touch the lives of those around him. I can't help smiling as I step away from the kitchen and look out the front door of the building. The sounds of the street are muffled. I see a group of homeless friends walk past, probably headed around the corner to get in line for the meal at the Rescue Mission. I wonder if any of Veasna's family members are hanging out on the street today.

Veasna says, "Every time I walk around the block or walk down to the corner, I see my family. Still selling drugs. Still on drugs. Still cheating people, beating people up, going to those parties. This is why I have to shine Jesus. It's personal. I had a guy come up to me and ask me, 'Do you remember me? I bought my first sack of weed from you.' It made me want to cuss. I brought so many drugs to this community, to my people, my friends, my family. I thought it was hope. I thought I had found an escape. Pop those pills. Drink that liquor. That's how you escape all the drama of living in the inner city. That's what everyone does. But now you know why I am so passionate about God. I have real hope. I know the antidote. I know the real escape. I have to share it."

We have a new hope. It isn't the temporal high of drugs or sex. It isn't the rush of quick money from selling Ecstasy. It is the hope of being loved completely—even though we are a mess and have sinned. I remember the day that truth took hold of me. It shook me to my core. And I know that it has shaken Veasna to his. All that the enemy meant to use to destroy Veasna, God has used to lift him up. His testimony is powerful. But the way he loves the people of the Tenderloin is even more powerful.

I leave the kitchen and make my way back toward the lunch room, taking a shortcut to the school. The people in this community, the kids in this school building, they are why Veasna does what he does. They are why he cooks meals and teaches and serves. They are why I do what I do, too. We have been shown a great love and been given a second chance at life. We want to share that love and those second chances with everyone in the Tenderloin. We are loving these people in the best way we can. Preaching from the pulpit isn't high on Veasna's list, but he preaches daily with his life, his actions, and his servant heart. A life changed is powerful, and you only have to look as far as the City Impact kitchen to find it.

~

George's Story

As told by Pastor Ralph Gella, SFCI staff member

George came to San Francisco from Michigan to escape problems with family and a failed marriage. He wanted to start over and find a better life. He ended up living in the Tenderloin in an SRO (a single room occupancy apartment). George worked at a nearby church as a dishwasher and became a member. In searching for purpose and a church that fit him better, George came to visit us one Sunday morning. He came in wearing a big cowboy hat and a three-piece suit. He sat in front with a big grin as he enjoyed the service. That was the beginning of our relationship and friendship.

George was touched by God's love and presence and became an active member at our church. George started hosting a weekly Bible study in his room. We worked with him to reach his neighbors. At one point, we had six to eight people coming regularly to his Bible study. George spoke highly of our church and loved Pastor Roger and Maite. He was a good friend to us all. Pastor Roger hired George to work in our kitchen and come on as staff.

George was a hard worker and was never afraid of any task. He even worked harder than the younger workers. He learned how to cook, clean, and run the kitchen. George was faithful and reliable and brought a good spirit to his work. We all grew in ministry together. One day, George got sick, and I sent him home. He did not come back when he was supposed to. I went to visit him and found that he had passed away because of complications from his diabetes. When I think of George's life, I see the faithfulness of God.

George came to the Tenderloin, hurting and having no purpose. He was just trying to live day by day. But the day he encountered God and God's people, George chose to connect and his life was changed. George now had a purpose in life. God was restoring him, rebuilding him as he served the community. If people only knew the hard work and sacrifice that George gave to City Impact and how he helped reach his community, they would have been amazed. If the people at the Rescue Mission dining room only knew who cooked their meals (at the time about 400 to 500 people a week) and how much care he put into them all, they would have been amazed.

George was a blessing to all the children at church. Many would run up to him, asking for candy. He always seemed to have some gum to give away. George's life was not a waste, he was a servant sent by God. To this day, I have never met anyone like George. He really was a great blessing to us all. God takes broken lives and the foolish things of this world to bring glory to His Son, Jesus. I believe everyone and anyone can be used by God and in that process, experience the abundant life in Jesus.

~

Chapter 2

Hearts Thrown Wide Open

A few streets over from our Jones Street building is an onramp to one of the main arteries in and out of San Francisco, Highway 280. When you take the 6th Street exit off of 280, you head straight toward the heart of the city. To your right, the flower market is crowded with delivery vans. On your left is the South of Market district, an area being revitalized by tech companies and young professionals. Traffic is always heavy. The streets are lined with businesses and shops. Within a few blocks, the look of the neighborhood begins to shift. The streets are a little dirtier. The shops have bars on the windows. You see homeless people on the streets. The theater district looms ahead as you turn left on Market toward Union Square, the city's main shopping area. Union Square is beautiful. Streets lined with high-end department stores and luxury hotels surround a central square. But to get there, you have to go through the Tenderloin.

My friend Ted, an investment banker, once pointed out that other cities try to show their best side first by hiding their poverty. Ted and his wife, Sara, moved to San Francisco from New York where the poor are tucked away in different boroughs. He said, "The first time I drove through San Francisco, I was caught off guard that it took me straight through the underbelly before I got to the beauty of the city." You go through the messiness of Turk Street before you make it to Fisherman's Wharf or the new Giants Stadium. The dark streets of the Tenderloin lead to the manicured homes of Russian Hill if you follow Jones Street up twenty blocks.

This city has never been able to hide its brokenness. It is in your face, asking you what you are going to do about it. Refugees looking for a safe haven, the homeless contingent, and patches of drug culture are woven in with posh neighborhoods. Hungry children and teenagers hardened by a rough life live only blocks from San Francisco's hippest companies. You can't escape it. You have one of two options: You can try to ignore it, or you can try to do something about it. Ted and Sara chose to do something about it. They came to the area with a sense of purpose and with a heart full of love for the children of the Tenderloin.

In 1997, City Academy was a fledgling private school with no budget and only a fervent prayer that God would help us reach the kids in the Tenderloin. My family and I started the school with less than dozen kids, a couple of teachers, a kindergarten class, and a truckload of hope.

If you walk into City Academy today, this thriving learning center seems a world away from that tiny beginning. I am aware of two realities when I step inside: the busy non-stop atmosphere of a growing school and a sense of peace. This place is a haven for the children. Home life for children in the Tenderloin can be painful. Some children come from single parent homes wracked by addiction. Others live squeezed into a one-bedroom apartment with numerous family members. Some kids look forward to school each day simply because they know they will get to eat a good hot meal. All of them long for a place to belong.

During a pivotal point in City Academy's history, Ted and Sara joined our work. Having been put on notice by the Fire Marshall that we needed to bring our current building up to code, the future of the school hung in the balance. Maite and I have always had a lot of faith and very little money. It seems to be the way that it works for us. Ted calls it bootstrapping—not the best business practice according to most chief financial officers. When we need money, we pray. When we are up against the wall, we fast. We know that God has the resources to do what we cannot. When Ted and Sara met us, we weren't a high-end nonprofit with a ten-year vision in place. We prayed in payroll for each payday. We weren't the normal fit for a person with Ted's financial know-how.

In the middle of our crisis, Ted and Sara were at a difficult point in their own journey They had found out they could not have children. They were letting to let go of their dream of having a family. In this season, God knit our hearts together. Ted and Sara saw beyond the grime of the neighborhood to the priceless treasure

25

of these children. Ted and Sara saw the needs that we faced trying to help these children. They saw the sacrifices that our teachers made in coming to work for us. They saw the dedication of the volunteers, who were willing to spend an entire afternoon with a single child to make sure that he or she understood how to read. They saw the transformation of the children, and they wanted to be a part of it. They poured all of their love into our kids at City Academy. Ted told me, "By having the opportunity to be tangibly involved with kids over time, we are getting a chance to be parents in a beautifully different way. The kids are receptive and hungry and want to understand their worth. The people of City Academy are making such sacrifices for these kids—visionary entrepreneurs who are completely and sacrificially committed to those they serve. It is inspiring."

They came alongside us in an authentic way, investing in the vision that God had placed upon our hearts. And in the way that only God can do, He began to layer miracle upon miracle. God meets us in unique ways when we pray and fast. He shows off His goodness and His creativity.

At the same time that He was inspiring Ted and Sara, He was moving on all fronts. Instead of simply bringing the building up to code, God inspired a team of builders, churches, and volunteers to gut the Jones Street building, giving us an entirely new school. Instead of reworking the existing classrooms, He gave us classrooms to house up to 300 students. Instead of limiting the number of students that could attend, Ted and Sara asked their friends to invest in the lives of our students, meeting tuition needs. Instead of closing the doors of the school, it was as if God flung open the doors, inviting more of His precious kids inside. He always does it better than we do.

The kids of City Academy know Ted and Sara. And they know love when they see it. When the couple arrived from New York and drove through downtown San Francisco, I don't think they ever imagined themselves becoming a permanent fixture in the Tenderloin. But because they have God's heart for His kids, they came and stayed—and they love the way that God is at work in their lives. It is hard not to want in on what God is doing. We couldn't be where we are today, without the faithfulness of God. One of the ways He showed us His faithfulness was through Ted and Sara's commitment and love.

Today, the halls are bustling with kids and volunteers. Bright pictures and posters line the clean white walls. On the second floor, the sound of working students in classrooms produces a steady hum. As I pass by a class, a teacher invites the students to work out the math problem shown on a large screen. Another class of children passes me single file in the hallway as they head down to the basement for reading time in the newly renovated library. "Hi, Pastor Roger!" A little girl wearing her burgundy uniform sweater and a big grin calls to me and waves as she walks by. I wave back. Now I am grinning. These kids and this school are my heart. Their voices fill my heart just like they fill the halls. I love the sense that in these rooms each day, the children are surrounded by hope and love. These students know that they always have a safe place to come here in the Tenderloin.

We have been built up and encouraged by Ted and Sara's presence. We have felt their unwavering belief in the children of City Academy. We are not the same people we were before they came. And they have been changed by us, too. Ted told me, "I've been involved in nonprofits and fund-raising before. But this is different. I'm passionate about the story of City Academy. I love telling the story. It has become our story." It is a long way from New York's financial district to Jones Street. But we are thankful that God led Ted and Sara through the city straight to us. Ted and Sara are more than investors in our students. The truth is they have become a part of our City Impact family.

~

A City Academy Story

As told by Vanessa Brakey, City Impact staff member

*S*o when are you leaving?" Those were the first words that ten-year-old Jane said to her new teacher. Jane was so used to people leaving her; it seemed to be one of the only constants in her life. Her father, teachers, and mentors had connected deeply to her and then been ripped from her tiny world. These losses deeply affected how Jane related to people her whole life. She was desperately seeking someone to connect with, love her, and stay around long enough to see her grow.

Jane appeared to be a normal kid with lovely long black hair. She had a joyful disposition that drew people to her. She started at San Francisco City Academy in her kindergarten year. Her mother had grown up in the Tenderloin and knew that one of the safest places in this area was San Francisco City Impact. As Jane grew, her brother and sister also joined her at SFCA. Her mother believed that SFCA was the best place for her children. Because of the hours her mother worked and the lifestyle she lived, Jane took responsibility to care for her younger siblings. Her young life was spent making sure that her sister and brother were taken care of. She did a good job. She saw that their homework got done, and she kept them safe at home.

As Jane grew into a pre-teen she carried a lot of responsibility on her shoulders. To her it felt like the weight of the world; but she hid her feelings well behind a bubbly personality, a beautiful smile, an above average GPA, and her excitement for God. Her graduation day was a sad day because she felt as if she was leaving her family. The staff at SFCA was her family—her one constant. The SFCA family never gave up on her, held her when she cried, and truly cared about her hopes and dreams. Now she had to leave her home for a new adventure—high school.

28

High school started like a beautiful dream. Jane's mask of joy and laughter led her into a whirlwind of popularity. She visited her SFCA family once in a while, gushing over her newfound friends, dances, and, of course, boys. Her SFCA "mommas" were excited for her but constantly reminded her to be careful of the high school traps: drugs, unsafe relationships, and cliques. She assured them that she was fine and that high school was awesome.

Time brought the violent collision of the truths of high school and the reality of Jane's broken past to a head. Her yearning to be loved and find true connection led her into unhealthy relationships with boys and friends. Slowly, Jane began to get into activities she never thought she would do, and it seemed as if each step she took was guided by the pain of her past. In the process, she pulled away from her SFCA "mommas." They didn't give up on her. They texted and called her often, expressing how much they loved and cared for her.

Unhealthy friendships led to drugs, which led to broken relationships, which turned to violent bullying, and eventually deep depression—all in one year of high school. One dark night, Jane decided that she did not want to live anymore. Her little brother called out to all of her SFCA family when he heard his sister's threats of suicide. He knew they would be there, that they would find a way to reach out. They did. They fought for her life.

Jane began engaging with her SFCA family again. She began online school and stayed connected at SFCA. She grew in her relationship with God as the women who had formerly been her teachers discipled her. Today, Jane is a minister to the children of the Tenderloin, helping with the local City Impact youth group and the children's Super Saturday program. Her passion for Jesus is so evident. That dark night is a distant memory for Jane now.

Seven years ago, Jane was a young girl who asked her teacher when she was going to leave. Recently, as a young woman, she told that same teacher, "I just want to focus on Jesus. It doesn't matter what career I pursue if I'm not right with God."

~

Chapter 3

A Life Turned Inside Out

You can't walk through City Academy without being drawn into the school office. It is the hub of all the school's activities. Sarah is our school office manager, and she is in the office early each morning. The Tenderloin always seems to move slowest in the mornings. The street wakes up gradually as storefronts open and people drive in to work. But inside City Academy, the school office is like a busy hive humming with activity. The office is a compact room with two workspaces and a main desk. A string of chairs is lined up under the window facing Jones Street. Colorful posters dot the walls. The office is already in full swing before the first child walks through the door.

This morning is a typical cool San Francisco morning. Even in summertime, our mornings invite the breeze of the bay to sweep through our streets. Through the blinds, you can catch a glimpse of the overcast morning and a few cars driving past. Our teachers and school staff have already hit the ground running. The office is packed. One of the teachers checks in with a cup of coffee in hand, before heading up to her class. A couple of volunteers are getting their name tags before they begin tutoring students. A student returning after a sick day still looks a little flushed. A parent needs to be called. The copier in the copy room is not working and needs to be looked at. Kids are filling the hallways, ready to head up to their classes for the day.

Sometimes I can't believe how far we have come. This thriving community was once just a dream. When I prayed twenty years ago for God to help us open a school in the Tenderloin, I didn't know what it would look like. I wanted to help the kids on these streets know the love of Christ and have a place in their neighborhood to learn, grow, and be safe. But God's realities are always better than our dreams. I didn't know that an army of volunteers would help us meet the needs of our at-risk kids. I didn't know that our kitchen crew would fix healthy meals to fill hungry bellies every day. I didn't know that the kids at our school would use the Bible stories we taught to teach their own families.

God always does things better than we can hope or imagine. This office is doing big work, changing lives every day. Loving His kids is what God told us to do. And we are doing it. I am still amazed at the people that God brings to partner with us. In the middle of all the chaos, Sarah is welcoming volunteers, putting out fires, checking temperatures, and is trying to get a little paperwork done.

Sarah may not seem like your typical office manager. She never imagined herself working with at-risk kids. She is a lovely young woman in her twenties who moved from a small town of 500 in Texas to the most crowded district in San Francisco. Forty thousand people live packed liked sardines within the one-mile radius of the Tenderloin. Their pain and heartbreak bleed out onto the streets every day. The atmosphere could not be more different from the quiet hometown that Sarah grew up in with its Southern values and well kept lawns. Sarah is a self-professed introvert. She likes to be behind the scenes and doesn't feel that she is a front-desk type of person. But during her year with the School of Ministry, she found living out of her comfort zone was exactly where God wanted her to be.

In her teen years, Sarah struggled with depression and body image. At her darkest time, she dropped to ninety pounds. The place she felt the safest was at home in her room by herself. She just wanted to sleep and be alone. Reaching out to others was difficult. Her closest friends were her two sisters. During this time of isolation, God began to work in Sarah's heart. She realized she needed Him. Despite growing up in a Christian home, she began to understand that all was not perfect. Her family needed Him too. God showed Sarah that isolating herself didn't help anybody, especially those who didn't know who He was. There were other families who needed God desperately too.

In the way that only He can do, God began to pull Sarah out of herself and show her how much the world around her needed Him. He wanted to use her to reach those people. Her fear and apathy toward others slowly began to morph into a passion for reaching those who are alone and needy. Her desire to be alone gave way to a desire to reach out to the hurting. She stepped out of the small circle of comfort she had built for herself and involved herself in serving others and even branching out to go on mission trips.

Sarah found her way to the Tenderloin while visiting a friend in the area. She and her friend had met on a short-term mission trip to Louisiana. During her visit, she stayed with her friend's cousin who happened to own a shop in the Tenderloin. Most tourists choose a nicer part of San Francisco to visit. Her friend encouraged her to go see Fisherman's Wharf or take a drive down Lombard Street, the windiest street in San Francisco. But Sarah couldn't get past the looks on the people's faces in the Tenderloin. The looks of hopelessness and fear. The Tenderloin was already affecting her. Her heart was moved by their neediness. Back home, people's troubles were hidden behind nice picket fences and regular church attendance. Here things were different. The people here wore their despair on their faces. The drugs, the poverty, the pain were all out in the open. She knew they needed Jesus. She wanted to be a part of telling them that they didn't have to be alone.

Once back home in Texas, Sarah began to search for a way to return to the Tenderloin. She looked for internships and jobs in San Francisco. She sent e-mails to various ministries in the area. Nothing came up. So she started going to a Texas community college and working, all the while searching for a way to get back to the West Coast. She couldn't seem to let go of that desire to be back in the Tenderloin, helping the people who had touched her heart on her visit. After five months, she gave up the search praying, "God, I'm done looking. You have to do it now. If You want me in the Tenderloin, You are going to have to make a way."

God answered in the creative way that only He can. While cleaning out her inbox, she found an e-mail from Sean, who worked in our School of Ministry. The e-mail was five months old. How had she missed it? How had she not seen this e-mail inviting her to come to the School of Ministry?

She emailed Sean about the possibility of attending the next School of Ministry term. He responded within hours. At her church, she received a prophetic word, confirming what God was already doing in her heart. He was opening the door for Sarah. She was going back to the Tenderloin.

Sarah was about to discover what happens when you turn your life completely over to God. He puts you in crazy situations and asks you to be more than you ever thought you could be. He invites you to do more than you ever thought you could do. From her quiet room in her family home, she was transferred and baptized into community living, rooming with other ministry students. She went from only attending Sunday services to living out daily service to the poor and leading groups in reaching out to the residents of the Tenderloin in the Adopt-a-Building program. Instead of being allowed to withdraw, she had to build relationships and engage. She became great friends with Rebecca, her roommate, discovering a kindred spirit in the middle of the Tenderloin.

Each School of Ministry student is asked to list the ministries where he or she would like to work within City Impact—the Rescue Mission, City Academy, the Thrift Store, or so on. Sarah made out her list. Her first assignment was the third pick on her list: City Academy. She didn't know anything about being with kids. She wondered how that was going to work. She was being challenged from all sides. Her fears, her anxieties, and her feelings of inadequacy all were all looming before her.

God always knows what is He is doing. Instead of being overwhelmed by being out of her comfort zone, Sarah discovered that her passion for helping others was the perfect fit for our school. Sharing her days with the little ones provided her with an opportunity to love and nurture. Sarah also discovered that she had a natural bent toward administrative work. While interacting with the parents, she felt her heart begin to change. Instead of judging them and how they were raising their children, she realized that these parents lived hard lives. They were working through incredibly difficult situations. They didn't have all the tools they needed, but they were trying their best to love their children. Each day they were on a path to becoming more and being more. The same path that Sarah found herself on. Her heart of compassion began to grow, not just for the kids but for entire families.

When Sarah's student ministry time was up, she wasn't ready to leave. She was torn. She loved her family in Texas, but she couldn't imagine not working with the families at City Academy. Her mom and dad gave her their blessing to stay on and continue working with us. It was all she needed to stay. Sarah stepped into the permanent role of office manager and hasn't looked back.

Sarah has come full circle. Her ability to be calm in the midst of chaos brings order to the office. Her smile and her compassion put parents at ease. Her connection with the kids comes from the fact that she loves them so much. She welcomes visitors and volunteers, and they are enveloped by her kindness. All those years ago, God drew Sarah out of her own pain and suffering by showing her kids like her and families just like hers that needed Jesus. And here she is, loving families in the Tenderloin, day in and day out. She is growing and changing every day along with them. Her comfort zone may be behind the scenes, but she is in the zone the God has for her. Breakthroughs come in all shapes and sizes.

Popping my head around the doorway, I see Alex, our volunteer coordinator, slide into his desk. The traffic is picking up outside the window. City Academy is in full swing, and the Tenderloin is finally coming to life.

~

An SFCA Summer Camp Story

As told by Noah Blakely

*O*ne *of the most encouraging sentences I have ever heard from an eight year old was "Now I know I have a daddy."*

City Impact's school, SFCA, has a summer camp every year for students that our teachers desperately try to reach here in the Tenderloin district of San Francisco. One of the students that came this last year to summer camp at our Fort Bragg Blessing Home was a young girl about to go into the third grade. I knew some of her brothers because they had attended our school in the past, so I knew her life was not the easiest.

This little girl lives in a single-parent home with a mom that is constantly being stretched by her children. You can assume that she is not getting the attention she needs from her overworked mom and nonexistent father. This little girl witnesses drug deals on the streets that she walks every day to and from school.

I imagined her without the father who is supposed to embody protection and strength for a child. I imagined her alone, witnessing the horrifying events that transpire daily in the Tenderloin. One example of the brokenness in this girl's life is that there is a sex club adjacent to her school. The only thing separating these two buildings is a brick wall. This is normal in the Tenderloin: prostitution, gangs, drugs, violence, and fear. Who is teaching this child the right things to think about herself so she will know not to follow the norm? Who is leading her? She has no father to tell her that she is worth more than selling herself for money. She has no father that cares about her to tell her that she is his little princess. She has no father to shield her eyes from the monsters that inhabit nearly every square inch of her community.

One of the things City Impact does in the summer is take children to our place at Fort Bragg. It gives the children a complete change of pace. We stay in a huge home with a bonfire pit. There are no drug deals or prostitution in sight. The children experience the outdoors and the beautiful California coast, and just for a minute, they can feel safe and rested. We spend nights bonding over games, stories, smores, and, my favorite, Jesus' redemptive power.

One evening I gave a message about God as our daddy and how He is so in love with His kids no matter what they have done. I was very clear that He is just waiting to wrap His arms around every one of us to protect us from the scary things that could harm us. I told the children stories about how big God is and how strong He is. As I closed my message, I looked around and thought, "Good, they didn't fall asleep."

Near the end of our stay, I overheard one of the teachers ask this cute little eight-year-old girl, "What was your favorite part of the trip?"

Her reply brought tears to my eyes then, just as it does now as I write this.

She said, "I know that I have a daddy now."

One little girl will forever know that she has a Daddy who cares, and loves her. She will know that He is always there for her. She will know that there is more than brokenness for her future. Every day she is in my class I get to tell her that her Daddy still sees and loves her.

~

Chapter 4

Coordinating Passions

I love seeing the young people who work in our front office. They are full of energy and passion. Sarah is printing out a name tag for one of our volunteers. Alex is on the phone. He is always on the move, connecting new volunteers with ministries where they can serve. When I was young, I was passionate about two things: being successful and Maite. If anything, I am more in love with Maite now than I was the day I met her outside my dad's liquor store. She is beautiful and kind. And she keeps me humble. When I told her that one of the volunteers said she wished her husband was just like me, Maite just laughed and said, "She doesn't know what she's wishing for." She is probably right. As I have stepped back from leading the ministry full time, we have gotten closer. I love that we get to spend our days together. We are still passionate about seeing revival come to the Tenderloin. But these days we are not heading in a million different directions trying to get there. We are walking out that mission together.

My passion about being successful has also changed. When I was younger, I was very focused as a businessman trying to provide and make a nice living for my family. Success looks different to me now. I am not concerned with how much money I have or how nice my house is. I am not concerned about excelling in my field or getting promotions. I am not worried that I won't be able to take care of Maite and myself when we retire. I know that we are in good hands. God has shown us over and over again how He can provide. When we pray and fast, He moves in greater ways than we can possibly imagine. Success to me is seeing God move, in His way and in His time. What I am most concerned about in this stage of my life is that God gets to do what He wants to do in and through me. That is true success. I want God to keep moving this ministry forward, not because it makes Maite and me look good, but because it shows off how good He is.

We want to walk through the doors that He is opening. We keep trying new doors. Sometimes they open. Sometimes they don't. But we keep trying. We keep looking for where He is leading. And we notice how He has answered our prayers time and again by bringing specific people to do specific work with us. In the early days of our ministry, everyone just did what needed to be done. We were leading Bible studies, prepping food, sorting clothes, washing dishes, and tutoring kids in math - all in a single day. There were no real individual tasks—we all jumped in and got it done. It was good knowing that anyone on staff was willing to fill whatever need we had.

But over the last decade, God keeps bringing people with a passion for the poor and a heart for following Jesus who also have specific skills. Teachers. Administrators. Builders. Computer geeks. Health care specialists. And while we appreciate their hearts to serve wherever they are needed, it is also a great thing to have someone who really knows how to work on Excel spreadsheets. Or to have a professional chef help design our commercial kitchen during a renovation. Or to have a licensed cosmetologist give haircuts at one of our outreaches. No one wants to have me cut their hair. Over and over again, we have seen God meet specific needs through specific people.

My friend Leslie, who came to us on a chance visit with her friend from Menlo Church, is one example. She is a former elementary school principal. Her entire life has been focused on education. With the help of her good friends and the backing of their church, they completely renovated our library. They outfitted it from top to bottom, filling it with books and creating a colorful, inspiring environment for our students. Her passion is educating children. She has poured her time, energy, and love into these children. Every week Leslie comes to our library to interact and read with our students. Who else has a school principal spending one-on-one time with their students every week? Our kids are all the richer for spending time with Leslie. And they are not the only ones being changed. Leslie has felt her own life grow and expand. Her love for Jesus and these kids is shaping her each week. Like me, she will never

38

be the same. God isn't just using us to help these kids. He is using these kids to fulfill His plan for our lives too.

Seeing people embrace their passion and use their individual skills when they volunteer is a great encouragement to us. It builds our faith and reminds us that God is in charge of recruiting here. He is the one that touches people's hearts and moves them to join us. Each person that God brings to City Impact, whether it is for a day, a month, or a year, has something different and special to offer. This is not a perfect organization. We are not perfect people. But God is choosing to use us anyway. And when we are all working together, loving each other, loving the community, doing what we know how to do best, we begin to look like the body of Christ. Hands and feet, eyes and ears, all doing their part to bring hope and love to our residents and to each other.

Volunteers breathe life into what we are trying to accomplish every day. That is why Alex is such vital part of our community. Coordinating people is no small undertaking. Alex is always busy. The phone rarely stops ringing and there is a steady flow of e-mails coming in to our website daily, asking about ministry opportunities. We love that people want to join in what we are doing. Alex is our first line of action. When someone calls or e-mails saying they would like to help in a specific way, he goes to work. He knows the different needs throughout City Impact. He hears from department heads and plugs in people where they are most needed. There is a constant need for help in the Thrift Store, City Academy, and the Rescue Mission. We are always thankful for extra hands. Alex is the person who finds the right fit for our volunteers. It is important work. Several of our full-time staff started out as volunteers and came through Alex's office. Alex knows that what he is doing is changing lives. It changed his.

Alex came to City Impact as a volunteer during a pivotal point in his own life. Just out of high school and starting college in downtown San Francisco, he was looking for something more. His relationship with the Lord had been growing and he was feeling challenged to give back. He wanted to serve in whatever capacity he could. He hadn't always felt this way about the Lord. He had always considered himself a Christian because his parents were Christians. But since he was raised in a home with just a nominal church background, he didn't really know much about God. By the time he was in junior high school he knew one thing, he felt lonely.

For years, Alex had been searching for a place where he felt accepted and wanted. In middle school, Alex went to a different school than most of his elementary school friends. So he looked to sports to find a group to identify with. But he didn't make the school baseball team he tried out for. One former elementary school friend was a part of a church basketball league, so Alex joined them, hoping to find a place to belong. The practices were on Sunday mornings and a church service followed. Since his ride to the practices always stayed for church, he was stuck going to the service. God seems to get us in the door in funny ways.

Alex wasn't excited about church. He thought church people were hypocritical, putting on a mask of goodness when they walked in. He thought worship was an anemic show. He especially wasn't excited about listening to someone speak for forty minutes. But over time, something strange started happening in his heart. Once at home, he would find the worship songs filling his head and he couldn't get them out of his thoughts. Before he knew it, he would find himself singing along. He would think, "Wait! I don't even like this song. What am I doing?" The words and melodies began to work their way into his spirit until one Sunday, Alex thought, "Man! I love worship." His love for music began to grow, and he asked his parents for a guitar. He spent his free time strumming in his room, exploring rock music. The worship pastor gave him some pointers. Within the year, Alex began playing on the worship team and learning chords.

But like most of our journeys of coming to know God, Alex was still searching. He didn't have the close relationships and friendships that he longed for. He still didn't feel close to God. Even though he was involved in worship, he felt left out of the close-knit community in his small church. He began to grow cynical. There had to more to life than potlucks and worship practice. He was looking for meaning. He was looking for purpose. Normal church life wasn't cutting it. Knowing God couldn't just be about church on Sundays.

It wasn't until Alex was in high school that he really began to think about the life of Jesus. A friend gave him a book about the revolutionary way that Jesus lived. He realized that Jesus wasn't just about potlucks and worship songs. Jesus was radical. He got in trouble by helping people on the Sabbath. He challenged the religious leaders of the day. He was for the poor and met sinners at their most broken. He loved them in their weakness and pain. He was a risk-taker. Jesus gave everything so that we could be free.

Alex felt that there was a disconnect between what he was experiencing at church on Sunday and how Jesus lived. Alex wrestled with wanting to follow Jesus completely. He wasn't sure about yielding his life to Jesus' risk-taking ways. In his church, emphasis was placed on making a good life for yourself and your family by making safe decisions. When Alex read the story of Jesus and the rich young ruler, he was challenged. Jesus wasn't asking for safe decisions. He wasn't just interested in following rules or creating financial security. Jesus wanted the young man's heart completely. Jesus wanted the young man to give up everything and follow Him. Everything.

Alex didn't know if he could give up everything for Jesus. His ambitions. His dreams. His desire to live the life he wanted. It scared him. He thought, "Maybe I'll go to school, make a lot of money, and then give up everything for Jesus." He wanted to be a good Christian, but he wanted to do things his way. He looked for every possible way to get around giving his life completely to God.

Alex found he couldn't get away from the thought that Jesus wanted his entire life. By the time he got out of high school, Alex was at a crossroads. He realized that Jesus wanted him to go all in. He made the decision to stop running. He wanted his life to reflect the life of Jesus. He wanted his friends to know Christ. He had a desire to help those who had less than he did. He began to dream about going to college to get a science degree and using that in a developing country. He wanted to go on a mission trip overseas. But even though Alex had big dreams, his daily routine didn't show it. He slept in until 3 p.m., attended City College at night, and played with his rock band.

Alex woke up one morning and felt like the Holy Spirit said to him, "I didn't give you this time to spend it this way." There was an urgency in his heart that he had never felt before. The time for his mission wasn't later. It was now. It wasn't overseas. It was in his own city. God wasn't waiting for him to give his life over completely after college. He wanted Alex to start taking risks now.

So Alex began to look for a place to serve. He found City Impact online. He called and talked to someone who told him, "Sure, we would love to have you." But weeks went by and he didn't hear anything more specific.

He began researching our different ministries and finally connected with my daughter, Michelle. She told him, "Yes, come in!" Within the next few weeks, Alex was in the office, doing data entry and folding envelopes. He was open to doing anything we wanted him to do. Whenever he wasn't in his college classes, he volunteered with us. He was delivering meals, answering phones, serving in the Rescue Mission, playing worship music for our services. The thing he was most passionate about was getting out into the community. His heart was drawn to the residents in the buildings. He went once a week on food deliveries, but he really felt that for people to know the love of Jesus, there needed to be more consistency.

When the Adopt-a-Building program started, Alex jumped at the opportunity to lead one of the teams. A specific team was assigned to each building in the program. The Adopt-a-Building program was launched as a hands-on way to minister to the residents in a specific area of the Tenderloin. Many residents are shut-ins. Others don't know about our services. Even more residents don't know about the life-changing love of Jesus. Each week, a group of volunteers and staff members goes to the building they have adopted. They deliver food, pray over residents, and develop consistent relationships.

Alex was on fire. This is exactly what he wanted to do. He was so excited, he could barely contain it. Here was the mission he had dreamed about. This was how he would give his life fully to the Lord. It was all making sense. At least, it was all making sense until his adopted building's manager told them they were no longer allowed to deliver meals to his building. Alex couldn't believe it. How could this be happening? He and his friends began circling the building in prayer each day, walking and praying for a breakthrough.

On the fourth day of their prayer march, Alex saw one of the building residents crossing the street. She was too far away to say hi. But he watched, horrified, as she was struck by a car. He ran over to her and bent down to see if she was okay. The driver jumped out of her car, and they called an ambulance.

The services manager from her building ran over to the scene. He had seen the accident from his office and came to see how he could help. In spite of the accident, the woman seemed fine. She answered their questions and didn't appear to have any injuries. Miraculously, she was uninjured.

When the services manager saw Alex, he asked, "Are you from City Impact?"

Alex said, "Yes!"

He said, "Man, we love the work that you are doing in our building and the food that you deliver to our people."

Alex took the opportunity to address the situation. "We were told that we couldn't serve your building anymore by another manager. We believe it was a misunderstanding. Is there some way that we can work with you to begin serving again?"

The services manager explained to Alex that the person who said they couldn't come was the property manager. He told Alex he would work it out. He did what he said, talked to the property manager, and gave Alex the go ahead to come back to the building. The second miracle of the day. The prayers of Alex's team and the goodness of God had reopened the door for ministry.

As the months went by Alex began to realize how great and how overwhelming the needs in his team's building were. He was giving his all as the team leader but it wasn't enough. There was so much poverty. So much hurt. So much devastation in so many individual lives. Seeing changes in the lives of the residents came slowly. The building had eighty residents, but there was only one Alex. How could he actually help them all? After a year, he was so discouraged he stepped away from leading the team. He felt like people were disappointed in him, and he was disappointed in himself.

Alex was completely overwhelmed by the scope of the need in the Tenderloin. For anyone who has worked for any length of time in the Tenderloin, this is a normal response. How can you not be overwhelmed in the face of such incredible odds? Alex knew that City Impact needed more than a few teams to help on the weekends. They needed hundreds of people to flood these buildings with the love of Christ. They needed a movement of the Holy Spirit. Alex's prayers began to change. Instead of praying just for the residents of his building, he began to pray, "God, will You help me to send Your church into action?"

Around this time Michelle reached out to him about a full-time job. City Impact had a position they wanted Alex to take: Volunteer Coordinator. She wanted him to follow up with and place new volunteers that wanted to be involved with City Impact. Alex had come full circle. Suddenly, he was in the position do exactly what he had asked God to let him do: mobilize the church. God was answering his prayer. He had seen his own life dramatically changed when he gave himself over to the mission God had for him. He was now in the place to help others on their own journeys of following God's mission and His passion for their lives.

God is always in the business of surprising us. Sometimes breakthroughs happen when we are the answer to our own prayer. Alex has been our volunteer coordinator for more than four years now. His ability to connect and place people in the different ministries is a blessing to us as we continue to grow and change. It is good to know that God is passionate about one thing: His kids. He constantly longs for our whole hearts and lives to be turned over to Him. The amazing thing is that when we finally give in to His relentless love, we see our greatest passions realized.

~

A Praise Report from a City Impact Volunteer

Happy Thanksgiving! We are so thankful for all of you and we pray blessings over you! City Impact and the work that you do over there, what God is doing has had such an impact on us! It has spread like a fire and God is doing amazing things in Michigan!!

After much prayer and Holy Spirit leading, we were guided to a trailer park north of us. It has 208 mobile homes and is full of poverty, brokenness, drugs abuse, and more. We took what we learned from Adopt-A-Building and we have adopted this park. We have gone in there twice with grocery bags of food and ourselves filled with God's love and knocked on doors, handing out food and getting to pray with people. It's been a beautiful thing! We will go back today and help a mom with three kids who has no electricity or food. We will bless her with a meal and groceries and go back in a couple of weeks, handing out winter coats.

I tell you all of this, not to boast but to humbly thank you for what you do at City Impact. Although my heart yearns to be in San Fran with all of you, my husband Jonathan has been led to start this here with the leading of the Holy Spirit. Revival is happening in our hearts and home. This is spreading through our church and making an impact. Thank you all! I sit in tears, thankful for my brothers and sisters, near and far, linking arms to love with the powerful love of Jesus!

We pray for you every day. I hope this e-mail brings encouragement to you. You are making a difference. We took what we learned and are living it out here. So so blessed. Although we aren't sitting together today, you are thought of. We thank God for you and are excited that our son, Austin, will be joining you for the summer program!!

God is so good. Overflowing thankfulness! God bless you all!

~

Chapter 5

A Joyful Life

This season of change has opened up more time for Maite and me to be together. Maite is my best friend. There is no one I would rather spend time with. During those crazy years of juggling careers, starting a new ministry, and raising kids, sometimes it seemed like we only saw each other in passing. Maybe the years flew by so quickly because we were so busy. Now as the ministry has taken shape and has been built up, we have more time to enjoy each other. And what we enjoy most of all is spending time with our grandkids. We are proud grandparents. We can't help ourselves. Each of our grandkids is beautiful and unique, and they are precious to us. As we have watched them grow and mature over the years, we have been reminded again that this is what we are all made for. We are all meant to grow up surrounded by love, to mature, and become the person that God created us to be. We were designed to become people who chase God and love Him back.

I was a late bloomer when it came to chasing God and His path for me. I was well into my thirties before I realized how much God loved me. I think I am still learning that. I have had to unlearn all the lies that I learned and believed from my childhood. I thought I was unlovable and unwanted. I thought I was a throwaway kid who didn't matter. Growing up believing those things affected my ability to love. It has been a decades-long process of healing. Maite's presence and God's steadiness and compassion have been the only things to see me through.

When I look at my grandkids, I am overwhelmed with thankfulness. They have always known the love of God. They have felt it through the lovingkindness of their parents, my own children. And this is a beautiful thing. Not every child is so lucky. A lot of our

46

friends here in the Tenderloin have had painful childhoods. They have suffered. They have experienced things that no child should ever have to experience. These experiences have rocked the very foundations of their souls. It can take a lifetime of recovery to get over it.

It is easy to judge someone you don't know who is strung out on drugs and passed out in the doorway of a worn-down shop. It is easy to walk by them without a second glance. We all need to remember, as we work with those who are hurting, that each one has a story to tell. I have had my heart broken by these stories more than once. It is easier to have compassion when you stand face to face with someone and hear, in their own words, what their life has been like. The cruelty and hardship they have walked through are overwhelming. It is harder to judge someone when you are crying with them.

As I leave the Jones Street building, I see a group of men walking toward the Rescue Mission. I follow behind them. Rounding the corner, I can hear the sound of singing echoing out the mission's open doors. There are a handful of voices singing praises to God. It is a good sound to hear. It is not a huge space, but big things happen here every day. We share our own stories of how God is at work in our lives and how He can work in their lives too. We don't want anyone to leave the Rescue Mission without knowing how much they are loved. It is love alone that sets us on the path of healing. We can't change people's hearts. That is the work of the Holy Spirit. But we can offer hope and a good cup of coffee. We do that on a daily basis.

I pause before going in. A large van is parked at the curb. Joe, one of our staff members, is unloading pallets of food that he and Pastor Ralph picked up from a local grocery store. Joe is grinning. It seems like Joe is always grinning. He has been working with us for the last couple of years. I throw up a hand, and say, "Hey, Joe! Did we get in a good shipment?"

He sets down a box of produce and waves back, "Hey, Pastor Roger! Yes, really good."

I grin back at him. You just can't help yourself. Joe's smile and his easy demeanor seem to bring out smiles in everyone around him. But I know he has grown into that joy over the years. He didn't always have something to smile about.

Joe was raised by his father in South San Francisco. His dad was a longshoreman who worked offloading huge containers from ships that docked in Oakland. When Joe was small, his dad lost both of his legs in a tragic work-related accident. Using the settlement from the accident, he bought a home in South City and, at the same time, sued for custody of his kids. Joe had been living with his mom up until that time. He was five years old when he moved in with his dad and brother and sister. As a black child in a predominately white neighborhood in the late 1960s, Joe didn't experience the prejudice in his neighborhood that you would expect. But what he did experience in that first year of living with his dad changed the course of his young life forever.

Joe was molested by an extended family member. One of the people who should have been caring for him and protecting him instead sent him on a downward spiral of hurt and despair. Being so little, Joe didn't understand what was happening. He was defenseless to stop it.

The foundation of learning he should have had as a kindergartner was completely undermined. He couldn't grasp reading or writing well. His small heart was too shattered. He had always been a good little boy, bringing smiles to everyone's faces. But soon his schoolwork faltered and he began misbehaving. His dad didn't know what was going on. He was busy struggling with his own recovery. For a man with a strong work ethic, he was at a loss with his disability and trapped in his own world of pain. He didn't know why Joe was acting out and just said, "Why can't you just behave?" Not knowing who he could turn to, Joe turned to no one. He swallowed his pain and kept quiet in his suffering. Like me, Joe was another small boy lost in the pain and disillusionment of abuse.

He made it through his sophomore year of high school without ever learning to read. He knew that his teachers shouldn't keep advancing him when the only words he could comprehend were "the" and "cat." Sitting through high school classes was excruciating. He was confused and angry. He began to drink. Alcohol fueled his violence at home. At seventeen, he left and never went back. He headed to the city and ended up in the Haight, the center of the hippy movement then. He walked the streets all night. Drugs were on the rise. Free love was the norm. Life for Joe became all about trying to survive and hustle. He couldn't read, so getting work was impossible. He spent the next four years living with the neighborhood "white witch," stealing food and money to get high. No matter how many drugs Joe took, the high never lasted long enough to take away his pain.

He thought maybe love could. Joe slept with both men and women, trying to find someone to fill the gap in his heart. When his first boyfriend threw him out after a year, he began selling his body to support his drug habit. By age twenty-two, he was doing his first stint in San Quentin. Alternating prison time and chasing down his next fix was the pattern Joe followed over the next twenty years. But God was already at work, chasing Joe. Even when we are lost and running from our pain, God does not let us out of His sight. While he was in prison, Joe began to turn to God. He remembered a bus from the Church of the Highlands that used to come to his neighborhood every Thursday night when he was a little boy. He used to get on the bus and go to Bible study. He didn't understand everything that he heard but he got the sense that God cared about him. Maybe God still cared about him in prison.

Using the Bible, he began to teach himself, slowly but surely, how to read. It was something he had never been able to accomplish in his childhood or life to date. God began to use him to encourage his fellow inmates. Several times, Joe felt impressed to tell different people a specific message. When he did, they looked shocked, and asked, "How did you know that was what I was praying about?" Even in his brokenness, God used to Joe to speak to others.

Each time he got out of jail, he tried to live right but without guidance and direction, he returned to what he knew, burglary and drugs. When he was in jail, he spent most of his time reading. He knew God was changing him but he didn't realize that he needed to give his life completely to God.

Joe says, "I just kept soaking in the Word, wanting what the Bible was telling me about, unconditional love. So that changed me. But I still didn't get it. I really didn't understand that I had to turn my life completely over to Him. But when I look back on how God was working in me, it is amazing."

One of the times that Joe was out of jail, he walked through the Tenderloin. He walked past the Rescue Mission and heard the music playing inside. He was on his way to go get high. Wondering what was going on, Joe went inside. Immediately, he felt God's presence. He felt the Holy Spirit impress on him, "This is where I want you to be."

But all he could think was, "No." He was still fighting the urge for the quick fix that drugs can give. Over the next ten years, he would come and volunteer at the Rescue Mission for a few months and then fall back into drug use. He would deliver meals and encourage people to come to the Bible study, but he was still naïve about the Christian life.

Joe thought once he became a Christian he would be a perfect person and that he wouldn't sin. It took years for him to realize that when you give your life to God, there is still a struggle within you and a temptation to turn to your old ways. The power to change comes when we ask God to be with us and help us in our weakness. Forgiveness comes when we sin and keep turning to God, asking Him one more time for His help and for His Spirit to change us.

Joe's journey has been a journey of falling down and getting up, of starting over and pressing in to all the love God has for him. It is a long way from the broken heart of a little boy to the path of healing that Joe has walked. But these last seven years have changed his heart. Joe realizes that God has more for him than pain and drugs and jail time. God has a unique plan for his life. Pastor Ralph has prayed for him for the last twenty years, and now Joe is Pastor Ralph's right-hand man with food delivery.

Joe says, "I was hooked on heroin and I was on methadone, and God released me from all that. And now, what I want more than anything is for the people that I hung out with to have what I have. I see these people all the time, and for the last several years, they've been seeing me. They keep asking me, 'How?' And I just keep pointing up, 'It's God. Believe me, it's God.' I tried to help people on my own, but God showed me, 'Just walk, they'll see you. Just walk.'"

And every day, the people of our community see Joe. He is on staff with us full time now. And he is walking. He is walking out the joy and hope that God has put in his heart even if there are hard days. He loves these people. They can sense it in how he talks to them and how he smiles at them. There is a reason that Joe smiles so much now. He has been set free. And that is our heart and prayer for every person here in the Tenderloin.

~

A Faith Story from a Tenderloin Resident

I was out for a walk one day, deep in thought, feeling so sad I couldn't stop crying. My tears were out of control. I sat down on the sidewalk and continued to cry. After a few minutes, I looked up at a man who would change my life.

He introduced himself and said, "You know that God would not leave you crying." He gave me his card and asked if he could pray for me. As we bowed our heads in prayer, I was distracted by voices in my head, laughing and taunting me, screaming that there was no hope and that God had given up on me. Yet, somehow, somewhere deep inside of me, I knew it was not true. So the following week I came across San Francisco City Impact Rescue Mission, a place to get a hot meal. While standing in line, I saw a pastor. After a short worship time and sermon, I gave my heart to Jesus and vowed to learn what I could about Him.

My faith was tested over and over, yet I held on. One day, I awoke and couldn't see. I was blind! Several years earlier, I was told that I had cataracts. Not having any insurance and because of other commitments, I put off surgery. Another reason I delayed was a negative experience my mother had thirty years before. She had eye surgery, but it was not effective. My mom fell into a deep depression that she never overcame, and because of this, she attempted suicide. She slipped into darkness and died at the young age of sixty.

I was diagnosed with cataracts at the same age as she had been. All I could think of was, "I am going to die young." That day I went home and I fell to my knees. I began to pray and really talk to Jesus. I prayed for a good five hours; yet, I didn't feel that it was enough.

So when I woke up that morning and couldn't see, I was angry. Once again, I thought that my faith was being tested. Yet deep down,

I didn't give up. I took on the day. I made phone calls—appointments with doctors. It took more than two years to get insurance and eye surgery. Let me tell you how I stumbled through that time as a seriously visually impaired person. A friend of mine loaned me a white cane. It was a blessing. I was able to get around. My whole world changed. The few people I knew turned their backs on me. Now, I had to deal with the loss of family and friends. Why? Maybe they were frightened or didn't want to be embarrassed by being with an old wrinkled blind lady.

Rejected yet again, I turned to faith and vowed that I would overcome. Those two years were so horrible. Bad things seemed to keep happening to me. Feeling so lost, I believed God wanted nothing to do with me. I was too damaged to be of any good to others. Death seemed like the only answer to my problems. I didn't understand this road that I had been given. I went to City Impact one Sunday and my heart was filled. I began studying the Bible. My faith was restored. I vowed to Jesus that I would look at everything through His eyes (at least the best I could). I hung onto my faith. There was nowhere else to turn. I had tried to commit suicide other times and hadn't succeeded. I began to believe that, yes, I did have a purpose in life. For each day I passed, I have been tested. Yet, I held on to my faith.

Being blind, I was able to be more in touch with my other senses. I faced rejection, prejudice and even hate. I was taken advantage of. I became disoriented and lost, often walking in the wrong direction. When there was no one to help me, I mustered up my courage, said a prayer, and continued on my way. I prayed for a guardian angel to help guide me to my destination and back.

Even though I stumbled often, I kept going to church, really wanting and needing to be around other Christians. I was introduced to a social worker. He helped me to get insurance and a doctor to help me. Because of him, as well as others, I came to know I was accepted into the church. I felt wanted for the first time. Their belief and prayers kept me, and still do, keep me strong. Especially when I become so frustrated I don't want to go on. My belief and faith are what got me here today.

Sometimes I thought I would never be happy. Each time I felt joy or happiness, it was taken away from me. I felt like someone was *saying that I do not deserve to be happy. Believing this, my faith became weak. So I withdrew and refused to feel happy even when I could have because I thought it would only be taken away from me. I became cold and so negative. I felt Satan had a hold of me. Then I had a dream that I was talking to God. He told me to "please hang on."*

Now, I know with all my heart it was no dream. It was real. I have had surgery on both eyes. After the bandages were removed, I was so overcome with joy and happy, happy feelings. When I got home, I spent the day listening to and singing worship songs. After a week, I went for a walk around and looked at everything—the drawing on the walls, the graffiti, green trees. I looked up at the most beautiful blue sky. No more shades of gray, no more black-and-white colors. I could see colors again for the first time in nineteen months, one week, and three days. I purchased a pair of glasses.

When I got home, I grabbed the Bible, opened it and read for the first time in such a long time. I now hope that for every person who comes across my path, a bit of faith, hope, and inspiration can enter into their life. Prayer works.

~

Chapter 6

A Firm Foundation

When you walk into the Rescue Mission, you walk into the heart of City Impact. Our heart that beats for the poor. This is the whole reason we are here. What started out with my family passing out sandwiches on Turk Street thirty years ago has evolved into something I never could have imagined. Every time we start a new program, it seems like another opportunity opens up for us to serve in a different way somewhere else. Maybe that is the point. God keeps showing us that He is not interested in our programs. He is interested in people. He wants to reach out to them in a thousand different ways. Sandwiches are good, but there is even more that He longs to do our community. If we keep our hearts open to His leading, He will keep opening new ways for us to minister.

Stepping through the open door of the Rescue Mission, I can smell the coffee brewing. It is always busy here. The clinic in the back of the building is prepping for the day. The social services crew are seated at their desks with their first appointments. The Morning Café is just concluding its breakfast service. A few of the people from the community are already cleaning up, putting away food, and pushing chairs back into place. Each morning, the mission offers a light breakfast, hot coffee, and a short devotional. It is a safe place for the community to gather and be built up. Life is hard in the Tenderloin, and the odds that our friends will survive on these streets aren't great. But there are pockets of hope to be found, and the Morning Café is one of them.

I see some faces here every day. An elderly woman who regularly pushes her handcart down Jones Street is resting while she eats a pastry. A homeless man who has been in and out of our doors for years sits in the back row. A young man who looks like he is trying to shake off the effects of whatever he drank last night sips a cup of steaming coffee as he pushes past me back out onto the streets. The Morning Café is a respite from the harsh reality of life in the Tenderloin. People can have a moment to rest their feet and regroup before facing their day. If they need help, they can get that too.

Pastor Ralph and Joe are unloading some boxes of groceries that have come in. Pastor Ralph manages the Rescue Mission and its many services. Some of this food will go down into the food bank and be distributed to the community. Each day, volunteers and students from our School of Ministry deliver food to the different buildings, homes, and single room occupancy units (SROs). These deliveries may be the only food some of the residents have for the day. Some of the fresh produce will be delivered to City Academy to feed our growing schoolkids. Another pallet of boxes will be set aside for the full dinner that is served at the mission tonight after our Bible study. We host a hot dinner every night.

More than two hundred people are served each week in the Rescue Mission. And those who are served are given the opportunity to come back here and serve their neighbors, too. They can volunteer at the mission themselves, setting up, cleaning, and serving meals. It seems that a different kind of healing takes place in their own hearts when they get a chance to serve those who are hurting like they are. It gives them a different perspective and a sense of purpose when they can take care of others and forget about their own problems for a few hours.

Maybe you can't relate to those in the Tenderloin. Maybe you have always had a warm meal and a good home. Maybe you have been loved and made to feel important and special. Maybe you have always known from the time you were a tiny child that God made you and that He has good plans for you. If so, try to imagine that you are living in a community of poverty where despair is a given. Put yourself, for a moment, in the shoes of one who walks these streets. You may be a refugee from another country or an addict. You may be a widow who can't seem to catch a break. You may be a child who is bused to a school in an unknown neighborhood and who has to pass drug dealers every time you walk home from the bus stop. You may be a teenager who ran away from home, bouncing from shelter to shelter, because you can't stand to be hit by your dad anymore. You may be an elderly man who is barely surviving on social security and a prayer. And you find yourself here on the corner of Jones and Turk Street.

Maybe you came here looking for your next high. Maybe you came here because you lost your job and you can't afford to get out of the city, and even if you could afford to leave, you don't know where to go. Who would take you in? You may not know where you are going to sleep tonight. Or maybe you have managed to squeeze your family of five into a pay-by-the-week hotel, and now you are not sure how you are going to feed them tonight. You don't know how to navigate the government systems. Maybe you are not sure how you are going to pay your bills with your minimum-wage job. Or maybe no one will hire you since you don't have an address to list on your job application. You never imagined this would be your life.

The emotions that rise up each morning when you wake up are overwhelming. Fear. Discouragement. Anger. Hopelessness. How are you going to make it? Where will you go? Is there hope in this place where sex shops are a dime a dozen? Is there any goodness to be found? Does anyone care about you at all? No one seems to meet your eye on the street. No one looks at you. You are alone. Ignored. Forgotten. Every morning is more of the same. Now imagine that you hear of the Morning Café. There is warm food and drink every morning. It may not solve all your problems but it is a start. It may not answer all your questions, but it is an answer to one question. Someone does care.

The good news that we serve up at the Rescue Mission is a two-handed gospel. The message you hear when you walk through our doors is that God cares about your soul and He also cares about your basic needs. The people in our community don't just need to hear God's truth; they need to see it in action. They need a living, breathing gospel that reaches them at the most basic level. God cares about the state of their heart. But He also cares that they have food in their belly and a chance to survive. The people who walk through these doors are people with real, palpable needs. A gospel tract slipped in their hand is not going to cut it. But real people living out the gospel among them, offering hope and a listening ear? That is a different story.

Dino oversees the care host program. His desk is tucked up against the wall near the back of the room. A young woman with long black hair sits across from him, leaning in trying to catch what he is saying above the noise in the room. People walk past his desk in a steady line. Volunteers are unloading crates, and patients are going into the clinic. Dino is oblivious to the scene around him as he talks to her. His focus is completely on this girl as he explains how we would like to help her. He passes her a couple of vouchers to our SFCI Thrift Store.

Dino and his six ministry students help meet the needs of the Tenderloin's residents in a physical way. Whether it is providing residents with food from the food bank or helping them navigate the county's government assistance programs, Dino and his team preach a hands-on gospel. Dino says, "What most people want is for me to listen to their story. They may need food or social security, but, really, when they share their pain with me, that is what makes the difference. Then I can share some of my story. When we share our pain, we form a connection." Dino knows what it is like on the other side of the desk. He has felt hopeless and lost.

Dino grew up in Oakland in the sixties with a house full of older brothers and one sister. His mom was married but a majority of the time she was raising her family on her own. Their neighborhood was being flooded with drugs and violence. Dino's mom was intent on keeping Dino, her baby, from the life that his brothers were already slipping into—the gangster lifestyle. The call of easy money, big Cadillacs, selling drugs, and manipulating women were alluring to most of the neighborhood kids. They wanted a better life for themselves. Gang life seemed to promise what they wanted. Dino saw his brothers reap the benefits with their fancy cars and penthouse living.

But God had his hand on Dino's life from a young age. His grandpa was a pastor. Even though Dino's mom wasn't following the Lord at the time, she would let Dino's grandpa take him to church when he visited them. Dino has a vivid memory of his grandpa taking him to a small prayer service and telling him to kneel down. His grandpa said, "Just pray. Thank You, Jesus. Thank You, Lord. Thank You, Jesus. Thank You, Lord." Knees pressed into the floor, eleven-year-old Dino repeated the words over and over again.

As the small group of church members began to pray in the Spirit, calling out to God and inviting Him into their midst, Dino was flooded with a tingling sensation from the top of his head down to the tips of his toes. Tears streamed down his face. He had never felt anything like it before. With the words, "Thank You, Jesus. Thank You, Lord," came a sense of peace and recognition. He knew this was the presence of God. Prayer was a powerful thing. This memory anchored Dino in the years to come with a sense that God was real. And, eventually, it would save him.

For years, Dino resisted the pull of the gangster life. Eventually, the lure of money and women was too much. By the time he was in his thirties, Dino was following in his brother's footsteps. He sold drugs. He ran with men who were willing to kill for each other, gangsters who lived by a code of violence and intimidation. Dino ended up in prison.

Meanwhile, his mom had given her heart back to the Lord and had a vision of Dino getting saved. In prison, Dino began to read his Bible and pray. He vowed to change his ways and enrolled in a pastoral program when he ended his sentence. He studied spiritual warfare and memorized Scripture. Dino filled his head with the truth of who God was, but the gang life still pulled at him.

Eventually, Dino slipped back in with his old friends and began selling drugs again. The never-ending cycle of pushing drugs and going to prison lasted seventeen years. Guns and violence were his norm. Run-ins with the law kept sending him back to the penitentiary. Each time he went back to prison, he found himself seeking that sense of God's presence he had known as an eleven-year old boy. He dove further into God's Word. He realized that he had to break the prison cycle, but he didn't know how. Each time he got out of prison, he would go back to his mom's house. Since she was getting older and needed more help, he wanted to take care of her in the same way she had loved and taken care of him. But being at home put him right back into the same neighborhood with the same temptations, the same friends, and the same struggles. He felt trapped.

Dino didn't want to leave his mom alone. But if he stayed in his old neighborhood, he knew he would continue the destructive cycle of drugs and prison time. His most recent time in prison he asked God, "Why can't I get it together?"

The parable of the farmer and the seeds came to mind. He was like the seed thrown on thorny soil. Each time his faith began to grow, he would get out of prison and the cares of the world, his temptations and struggles, would choke out the truth. He needed good soil to grow his faith. "I had little faith, and the world was choking the Word out of me."

A turning point came when Dino saw one of his good friends who had turned his life around. He had left the drug life. He had gotten married and had a family. He had a good job and was doing well. And it tore Dino apart. He wanted that life for himself. Every time he walked by a restaurant and saw a family sitting down to dinner or people walking in the park enjoying themselves, he was filled with anger and despair. The thoughts that filled his head were negative and toxic: "It's too late for you. You will never have what these people have. You are too old. You are black. You have wasted your life."

Dino was desperate. He felt the Holy Spirit speak to him and say, "If you don't get out of here you are either going back to prison, you will kill someone, or you will die."

Dino shoved his clothes into a paper bag and went to the Bart station. He was going in search of a new life. He headed to the Tenderloin where one of his old friends lived. For eighty-two days, he lived in shelters, not knowing what he was going to do or where he would find his next meal. But he knew that God had spoken to him and he was listening this time. He wasn't going back home. On one of his daily walks in the Tenderloin, while looking for some way to spend his time before the shelter opened for the evening, he noticed a group of young people going in and out of the Rescue Mission. They looked different. They acted different. There was joy on their faces. Dino recognized that look. It was the look he felt on his own face when his grandpa taught him how to pray. He wanted that look, that feeling of joy.

It was 2012 when Dino came to the Rescue Mission for the first time. He was a fifty-four-year-old man looking for a new life and a path of faith. And he saw that path leading straight into the mission. He began serving alongside us. He went with a team on Sundays to serve food in the surrounding buildings with the Adopt-a-Building program. He found housing nearby in one of the single room apartments through a county program. He didn't have a lot of money, but he found good soil to grow his faith. He didn't have a job, but he wasn't selling drugs. The truth of who God is was changing Dino. He left the gangster life. God was healing his heart and mind. As Dino prayed and drew closer to God, he was delivered from all the anger and violence that consumed him. He began working with a ministry student at City Impact who was trying to start a Social Services department in the Rescue Mission. Things in Dino's life seemed to be falling into place.

Each time he sat across the desk from a hurting person, he saw himself in their eyes, broken, angry, and hurting. Each time he sat with a young girl who was selling herself for drugs, he wept, recognizing how he had given up his own life for drugs. Each time he walked a homeless person through the process of trying to find their own home, he saw his own struggle to find his own place. It was as if every heartache and despair he had felt were being mirrored back to him in someone else. But now it was different. He was sitting on the other side of the desk. He was sitting on the side of hope. The side of fresh starts and healing and new life.

Now, he has a message for each person that he meets with. "It is not too late. It is never too late. If it is not too late for me, it is not too late for you. If there is hope for me, then there is hope for you."

Dino is a changed man. And the change in him is changing others. He is a powerful man of prayer, and he lives by the chapters of Scripture he has faithfully memorized. He has that look of joy and compassion that draws people to him. A man walked up to him on the street the other day, and said, "Dino, you don't remember me . . . but you saved my life."

The presence of God that Dino felt so strongly as a young boy is overflowing in him now, pouring out onto everyone around him. Sometimes God has to lead you to the Tenderloin to give you the life that you are destined for. This place that is filled with hurting can be a place of healing. If you ever doubt that, think of Dino. He is living out his faith, moment by moment, bringing light into a dark place by handing out clothing vouchers and canned goods, with prayers and words of hope. I have a feeling that this is just the beginning for Dino.

~

A Thank You Letter from a Tenderloin Resident

To Whom It May Concern:

I first met Dino Powe at San Francisco City Impact in April of 2013. I was in need of food, emergency shelter, and positive direction. Dino went above and beyond to assist me in acquiring these things. Not only did he help me find the resources I lacked, but he actually spent time taking me to the various offices and locations to get the assistance I needed. Dino also invested his personal time and money mentoring me and helping me regain a sense of self-worth.

I've never met anyone so excited about helping another individual, especially one he barely knew. His care for others goes above anything I have ever seen before. Dino puts an immense amount of care into all the work he does. He is not satisfied until the person he is helping has everything they need to make the next step in their life. I am truly grateful to have Dino in my life, and I would not be where I am today without his unparalleled care and assistance. Dino started as my mentor but is now a friend that I will treasure for my lifetime.

~

A Rescue Mission Story

As told by Kent McCormick, City Impact staff member

When I met Leo in 2012, he was struggling with severe depression and had no hope his life would get better. He attended our Rescue Mission meal services on a regular basis but didn't talk much. At fifty-two years of age, Leo had struggled with decades of addiction and had lost a great deal of time and many relationships to his struggle. He occasionally shared about his inner pain and regrets. He often expressed that he felt like he had no purpose and nothing to look forward to. I often sat and talked with him about Jesus and offered prayer, but he was very resistant. After a few months, I asked Leo if he would like to volunteer in our Carehost Program. Through this program, we empower and train community volunteers to lead weekly grocery pantries for the low-income buildings in the area. Leo, who lived a few blocks away in a low-income housing complex for senior citizens, reluctantly agreed to give volunteering a shot.

In the months that followed, we witnessed a change in Leo. He gained so much confidence and found great joy while serving the residents in his building. He quickly began volunteering at every possible opportunity. He was able to connect with a part of himself that he thought he'd lost long ago. His big smile would brighten the Rescue Mission. He quickly became our most reliable and passionate carehost as well as a dear personal friend.

Though Leo found a joy and purpose in his service, he still fell into his old addiction pattern and this led to severe, intermittent depressions. He loved helping others but felt empty and ashamed. In the summer of 2013, he came into the Rescue Mission to pick up his pantry load and we all noticed that he wasn't his normal vibrant self. He asked me if we could talk for a moment, and I agreed. After heading down to

64

our food bank, so we could speak privately, Leo explained that he was struggling with very dark thoughts. He told me that he planned to kill himself later that evening. Leo felt that he couldn't continue living with the pain of growing old with so many regrets from the past. He believed that he was too old to change his life, and he wanted to give up.

We talked for hours, and I pleaded with him to surrender these things to Jesus. He realized he was at the end of his rope. After we walked through the gospel together, Leo gave his life to Jesus. Through the prayers and the tears, Leo finally found what he needed. For the first time in his life, he was able to surrender his pain and regret and let God take away his burden.

"Come to Me, all you who labor and are heavy laden, and I will give you rest. Take My yoke upon you and learn from Me, for I am gentle and lowly in heart, and you will find rest for your souls. For My yoke is easy and My burden is light." Matthew 11:28-30

In the months and years that followed, Leo was transformed. He continued to serve faithfully at the Rescue Mission and quickly became a power force in his building as well. He found victory over his addiction through our recovery groups and divine intervention. At every opportunity, he shared with others about the God that transformed his life. He eventually began to disciple people in his building and brought them with him to serve at the Rescue Mission. One of his helpers, John, also grew to be a faithful presence here at the Rescue Mission. Leo met with me regularly, and we'd walk through the Bible together. His joy and passion were an inspiration to everyone he came in contact with.

Fast forward to December 19, 2014. John, Leo's good friend, came into the Rescue Mission looking very sad. It was rare to see Leo and John not together. The two had grown to be inseparable. Confused, I asked John where Leo was. He explained that two nights before, Leo had been shot to death while walking home from the store around two o'clock in the morning. John said he was caught in the crossfire as one drug dealer attempted to kill another. Leo died before the paramedics arrived. I and many others were totally shaken by this news. Devastated. We had lost a dear friend and a brother in Christ to a senseless act of violence.

Despite our sorrow, there is room for rejoicing. Coming up on the anniversary of Leo's death, we find comfort in the fact that Leo is in the presence of our heavenly Father right now. He was saved that day in the food bank. He could have very easily ended his life that day, but God chose to save him instead. Now he lives in eternity. His memory and his influence outlive him. Praise God for this man and all the lives he impacted.

~

Chapter 7

Healing Bodies, Healing Hearts

The line of people headed toward the back of the Rescue Mission is growing. A young mom jiggles her baby on her hip to quiet him. Behind her, an older man with white curly hair shuffles forward with a limp. You can tell that his leg is bothering him. City Impact Health and Wellness Center is one of the busiest destinations in our Rescue Mission. The exam rooms have been prepared and are ready for the day's patients. Open weekdays, the clinic sees a constant influx of patients needing medical and dental care. Some have made appointments, and others are walk-ins off the street. Slowly, the clinic has become known in the neighborhood as a place that wants to help and heal. We have a rotating volunteer staff of twenty-seven doctors, six dentists, and fourteen nurses. This is a miracle center in action.

If you have a job with benefits, then you tend to take a medical care for granted. If you get sick, help is a phone call, a doctor visit, or a prescription away. But for our residents, good medical care is never a given. Some have never had insurance or a regular doctor. It is hard to navigate the health care system when you are homeless or when you are a young father struggling to support your family. People can go years without having their teeth cleaned or getting a general physical check-up. For the elderly, just getting to the doctor can be an overwhelming obstacle. For them, this clinic is an answer to prayer. For us, it is an answer to the dream God put in our hearts to minister to this community body, mind, and spirit.

When you look into the different faces of those who come into the Health and Wellness Center, one thing that strikes you is the tiredness etched on   people's faces. The stories written in the stoop of their shoulders tell of their struggles to survive in a harsh environment. Drug addiction and malnutrition aren't out of the ordinary. Years spent in poverty can wear down the body. From poor nutrition to the aches and pains of sleeping on the street to the ravages mental illness, our doctors see it all. They see faces spent in years of hard living and faces that have experienced things most of us can't imagine. When someone comes to you in physical pain, you want to help them heal. You want to bring physical comfort as well as comfort for their soul. It is hard to accomplish one without the other.

The clinic is one of the practical ways that we walk out God's love for this community. Basic medical care is an essential. But basic medical care given by someone who not only cares about the conditions of their bodies but also the conditions of their souls is transformational. Seeing doctors laying hands on their patients in prayer after an exam is something you don't experience at every medical office. Seeing a nurse with her arms wrapped around a hurting young girl or with her head bent near a baby in a stroller, whispering a prayer over the little one is a normal occurrence here. The health-care workers here are ministering to this community. Their actions speak as loudly as a well-thought-out sermon. The tender care they give shouts that God loves the least of these. They offer dignity and hope to those who need it most of all.

Our head nurse, Alyssa, is headed out the door for a house call. She loves being in the field. Many of our residents can't leave their apartments. Alyssa's heart is not only geared toward the study of medicine, it is geared toward reaching out to the poor. She isn't put off by the scent of unwashed clothes or rundown apartments. These apartments are the homes of the people she loves. One of our volunteers recently went to deliver food to an elderly gentleman who can't leave his apartment. There wasn't much decoration or comfort to be found in his sparse studio. But Alyssa's name and number were tacked on his wall. That is what love looks like.

The dedicated men and women who volunteer here on a regular basis don't underestimate the mind and body connection. Many of them feel their call to medicine was a dream that God put on their hearts. Their desire to be a doctor or nurse is directly linked to their desire to help others. And they are willing to let God use them in whatever capacity to minister to the minds, souls, and bodies of our residents.

One of the things I have realized in my years here on Jones Street is that dreams are hard work. Putting feet to our faith isn't a small undertaking. Our clinic manager, Alex, can attest to that. He works hard to keep the volunteers organized, to obtain grants, and to keep the shelves stocked with supplies. His keen business sense and ability to run this arm of City Impact are invaluable. You may wonder how we could find someone as talented or committed as he is to work in a nonprofit and join us in our inner city work. We didn't. God led him to us. Somehow God keeps bringing the right people at the right time with the right abilities to do the work that He has prepared in advance to be done. We pray and He answers. Sometimes the answers come quickly. Sometimes we pray for years. But He always gives us what we need at just the right time.

Alex didn't originally come to City Impact to work with the clinic. He got an e-mail about our Adopt-a-Building program being launched and came the first Sunday. He wasn't put off by the sights and smells of the rundown buildings or apartments. He wasn't discouraged by the people who closed doors in his face or didn't want to talk to him. To him, reaching out to the poor and loving the broken was what loving Jesus was all about. It was the bedrock of his faith. Ever since he came into his own faith of loving Jesus, loving the least of these was a part of his journey.

Alex's parents escaped Cuba when it was taken over by Communism. His parents lived in New York only a few years before he was born. His mom was a strong Roman Catholic who prayed for him every day. He was seventeen when she passed away. Alex had an encounter with the Lord when she died. Alex never doubted that God was real, but he just wasn't ready to give his life to Him. Sometimes God chases us for years before we recognize that we want to chase Him back.

Life for Alex was about partying and living in the moment. It wasn't until his later college years that Alex felt drawn to reading his Bible and wanting to know more about God. He graduated from college with a degree in international business, and eventually found himself working in Singapore. There he first acknowledged that he wanted God to be in charge of his life. He wanted to know more about this God of love. He needed to be discipled. He thought he would be in Asia for only a few years, but God had other plans.

When Alex relocated from Singapore to Hong Kong, he attended a church planted by Jackie Pullinger, an English missionary who had begun a work in the opium dens of Hong Kong's Walled City. The church's leadership was made up of former heroin addicts, drug lords, and prostitutes. These leaders had experienced the freeing power of the Holy Spirit and their lives had been turned inside out by the power of Jesus. The church met in small clusters, going out into the streets, ministering to the lost and broken. From this beginning foundation of Alex's faith, he experienced the power of God at work in the lives of those who needed Him most.

When a new job required Alex to relocate to China, he met the underground church there. His faith was further nurtured and strengthened. By the time Alex returned to the United States in 1999, he had been abroad for almost a decade.

He moved to Colorado and worked with an organization focused on getting the church to engage with unreached people groups for six years. They targeted what's called the "10-40 window," named for degrees of latitude on the globe where the largest concentration of those whom the Gospel has not reached live. Alex's heart and faith continued to be shaped by God's heart for the poor.

When he returned to China in 2006 for a new position, he formed a small church planting group that was birthing churches among the poor and the beggars of the community. It seemed that each time God moved Alex, He had him rubbing elbows with the broken. Alex was drawn to these people. He found them beautiful.

The journey that God led Alex on wasn't easy. After a few years of bouncing around different in jobs with General Electric on the West Coast, he was struggling to recover from a broken marriage. It was a time wrapped in sorrow. Some dear friends reached out to Alex and invited him to come to Haiti. The earthquake had devastated the country, and they were trying to get a hospital back into operation to help in the relief efforts. The hospital hadn't sustained earthquake damage, but it had been shut for financial reasons. Alex told his friends he would join them for a few weeks. He ended up staying two years. During these pivotal years in Haiti struggling to get the hospital running, he began to consider a career change to the medical field.

Haiti reorganized Alex's passions. He no longer wanted to work in the international business field. When he came to the Bay Area from Haiti, he looked for work in the medical field. He also looked for an inner city church family with a heart for the broken. When he received the e-mail from a friend about the first Adopt-a-Building outreach, it was right up his alley. When he arrived that day and joined the team going into the building's SRO's bringing food to the shut-ins, he connected immediately. He became the first volunteer building leader for one of the buildings. It was a natural fit for him, and he loved connecting with the residents on a weekly basis. He understood their plight. He knew brokenness. He was healing himself.

During the year and a half that Alex was a building leader, he also connected with my son-in-law, Clint, who had started a small emergency clinic in the back of the Rescue Mission. The clinic was open at odd hours and some weekends. Clint wanted to expand the clinic and knew he needed a plan.

It always amazes me to hear the hurdles that our team members have experienced before they arrive at City Impact. God is creative in how He works and knits our hearts together. Knowing of Alex's hospital background, Clint asked to Alex design the clinic's strategic plan, the budget, and to help get it off the ground. They wanted to open the clinic to the whole community on a daily basis. When they received their clinic license, Clint asked Alex if he would be willing to come on staff. They had one doctor, two nurses, and a dream. And now that dream has come to pass. It is a dream that sees people becoming whole—body, mind, and spirit. It is a dream that is growing and changing every day as our doctors and nurses interact with the community, bringing healing in a thousand ways.

Alex knows the hearts of the people who walk through the clinic doors. He has seen their pain a hundred times over as he has visited with them in their buildings. He has heard their stories and shared life with them. He connects with the care providers each morning in prayer before the day begins, reminding them of the true purpose of the clinic. He says, "Many of the residents we're caring for are actually living in hell, which is not living at all. They're walking alone and separated from God, and living in torment. So my goal is to remind our providers that this is their primary goal—to love the hell out of people. Literally."

The power of God's love is what does the real work. In Alex's heart. In the hearts of the providers. In the hearts of the residents. The clinic's sole purpose is to bring the love of Jesus close, through medical care. With a kind word. A heartfelt prayer. A listening ear. A hug. With a daily presence in our community. The clinic is the breath of heaven here on earth. And that is the kind of breakthrough we all want.

~

A Letter of Hope

To whom it may concern:

Two years ago, I had so much emotional and physical pain. I did not want to live. I tried to jump off a freeway overpass. I stepped off the overpass at 2:30 a.m. and something picked me up and laid me gently on my back on the sidewalk. I sat up, looked around to see who had stopped me, but no one was there. There was not a person within two blocks from me.

The next morning, I met a man named Christian and I told him what had happened. He asked me if I wanted to go to have free coffee and donuts, but I would have to sit through a short service. No problem. I grew up with my grandfather, who was a monster.

We went and I met Dino. He provided me with clothes and prayed with me. He offered me resources to help with my problems. I returned two to three times a week and each time Dino would bring a couple of people to form a circle. We held hands and they prayed for me. It gave me the strength to hold on for the first time in two years. I felt like someone cared. It gave me hope.

Today I have my own place. My Social Security insurance was finally approved, and I am looking forward to the future. I went to get coffee this morning to tell Dino thank you and gave a progress report because he was the only one I felt truly cared. I want to thank the Lord for sending Dino my way. Without him, I probably wouldn't be here. I believe Dino will have a special place at God's side. He has dedicated his life to helping those who have problems. God will bless and reward him. I had strayed from God during my troubles and the people involved in this made me realize I needed to get with God. Dino prayed with me and when I gave my life back to God things, started to get better.

It's time to take the next step. See you in church Sunday, Dino, and thank you for being there for me as well as caring. You helped save my life. May God bless you and all the people who ministered through the Word and especially the music.

Alex A.

Alex Q.

Alyssa

Bethany

Dino

Eric

Joe

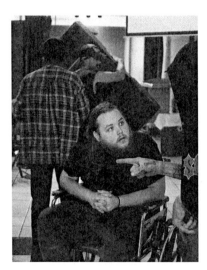

Kent

Laura

Manny

Matt

Michelle

Pushpa

Ralph

Rebecca

Sarah

Kristin, Chris,
Leslie

Ted and Sara

Terry

Veasna

Maite, Chris, Roger, Michelle

Roger with family

Chapter 8

The Turk Street Breakthrough

The San Francisco City Impact Thrift Store is busy this morning. After a recent renovation, its fresh white walls and weathered wood flooring invite new customers each day. Buckets of newly opened flowers frame the door, bringing spots of color and beauty to this little patch of the Tenderloin. I am not here to look for anything for myself this morning. My son, Christian, says I dress like the Chinese Johnny Cash. I wear a wide variety of black. I have what I need. But my family and our staff have been blessed over and over by the items donated to this store. The racks of gently worn clothes and displays of used housewares meet a need in our community.

I breathe in the smell of new paint that still lingers in the air. Furniture is grouped together at the back of the store along with different electronics. The beautiful arrangements of clothes on the walls make this space look more like a fashionable boutique than a common thrift store. I shake my head and grin. The amount of time and care that our staff and ministry students put into bringing dignity and comfort into this space is amazing. Their love shows in the way they interact with the residents. Their care for this community is echoed in their hard work and how they keep the store clean and well stocked. You would expect that down the street at Macy's in Union Square. At a secondhand store in the Tenderloin? Not as much.

Customers trickle through the door a few at a time to check out the latest additions. A young mom picks through one of the racks as her baby sleeps in a stroller. An older Asian gentleman is eyeing a warm coat, checking to see if the zipper works. We get daily donations of clothing and housewares here. It is always interesting to see what comes in and who will be able to use it.

One of our ministry students at the counter rings up a bouquet of bright white-and-yellow daisies. Flowers might seem like an extravagance in a place where poverty is the norm. But the flowers are one of the things that sell first in the Thrift Store. Maybe that's because their beauty is needed most in a place where hope runs thin.

We always look for ways to bring hope to the residents in the Tenderloin. We want to share the good news of what Jesus did for us when He died on the cross. That is the most important way that we can serve this community. But that message is best delivered when we meet people's physical needs. It is hard to listen to how much someone cares about you when you haven't eaten for a day or two. It is hard to concentrate on what God wants to do in your life when you can't find a way to keep out the winter cold.

Love can look a lot like a jacket and some hot soup. So much of what we do on a daily basis is meeting basic needs. When someone shows you love by caring for your body, you are much more willing to listen to what they have to say about your spirit. When Maite started the first thrift store years ago in an old strip club, it wasn't because she wanted another project. She would tell you that I am enough of a project for anyone. She started collecting clothes and household items because people in the Tenderloin needed clothes and household items. Sometimes the simple things make the biggest impact. A clean blouse. A pair of pants without holes in the knees. A sturdy pair of shoes. These daily miracles can make a world of difference in someone's life.

It can take years before a Tenderloin resident feels like we truly care. People don't trust easily. They have been hurt and taken advantage of so much in the past. They have known the deep heartaches of life. Often, their lifestyles and choices aren't the best. Many of them are trying to escape the pain of life through drugs and alcohol. Crazy things can happen here every day. It requires a different mindset in ministry when you don't know if the next person who walks through the door will be high or might try to steal some of the merchandise. Fights have broken out over a pair of shoes. There are moments when we feel like we are not making a difference in the face of so much hurt and despair. But the truth is that we have cracked open a window into the soul of one person every time we show loving-kindness. We are here to show love. Plain and simple.

82

Jesus came to minister to the sick, not the healthy. He saw the sin and depravity of people surrounding Him. He loved them anyway. We want to do the same. We are going to keep on showing up. We are going to keep on passing out cups of coffee and words of hope. We are going to keep offering up prayers on behalf of the forgotten. This store is a place where those things happen. Little miracles take place here every day. The fact that we are in this building on Turk Street is a miracle in and of itself.

I never take miracles lightly. This building is flooded with grace from top to bottom. The top floor of the building hosts the TL Made studio. TL Made is a social enterprise where resident Tenderloin artists produce beautiful artwork. Their hand-tooled leather crafts, handcrafted jewelry, t-shirts, and bath products are sold online to benefit this community. Seeing the creativity that flows out of that small space is beautiful. There are days when the whole building smells like the lavender candles that they are pouring upstairs. There are also two apartments in the building that house staff members and their families. This is a huge blessing due to the housing shortage in San Francisco. The Thrift Store occupies the ground floor. In the basement, we run a live-in drug and alcohol recovery program. Every square inch of this building is being used. Used for the beauty and purposes that God ordained. He never ceases to amaze us with His generosity. And whatever He gives us, we want to use to its fullest.

When I first noticed this small building on Turk Street, we weren't planning on buying a building. The bottom floor had recently been used as a store front church. The church had folded. It is hard to keep a ministry afloat on these streets. The rent for the ground floor was $4,000 a month. We were looking for a new home for the Thrift Store, and seeing that vacant space got me thinking.

On that cold afternoon, three years ago when I passed by this building I stopped and peered through the front window. I saw a dingy room that needed some cleaning, but I have never been put off by dirt and grime. I saw possibilities. We have never taken on a project or building that didn't require a lot of elbow grease and hard work.

The "For Rent" sign listed the number of the owner. I rubbed my forehead with my hand. The thought crossed my mind: "If I'm going to pay $4,000 a month for rent, I might as well buy the whole building and get the floors above to use for other ministry purposes." Over the years, I have learned that if I am going to dream, I might as well dream big.

Buying real estate on the San Francisco Peninsula is no joke, but I think God must have a good sense of humor. If God owns the cattle on a thousand hills, then He must also own quite a few buildings in the Tenderloin. There is no reason why we should own any real estate at all other than the fact that He wants it to be so. I am going to keep asking for His direction. I am going to keep seeking His will. And I am going to keep knocking on doors. Doors won't open any other way. As long as He opens doors, we are going to keep walking through them. Leaning up against the building, I punched the number of the owner into my phone.

It rang a few times. The owner picked up the line.

"Hello?" A woman answered the phone in a clipped, high voice.

"Hi! I am Roger Huang with City Impact. We have the Rescue Mission down the street from your building on Turk Street. I saw your room for rent in your building."

I paused. Nothing. I took a deep breath and kept going.

"So anyway, I would like to buy your building."

There was a sharp intake of breath on the other end.

"No. I am not selling it. Good-bye."

With that, she hung up. No "Thanks for your interest." It was just a very rude exchange.

"So much for buying this building," I thought. I headed back toward the Rescue Mission. I told myself, "I gave it a try. What more can you do?" But I couldn't get it off my mind. I tried to let it go for a couple days. But the thought of that little building with all of its possibilities kept popping into my head. I decided to call again.

In my office later that week, I dialed her number again.

She answered in the same manner. Not excited in any way to hear from me.

84

"So, this is Roger Huang again. I am still interested in buying your building. I am thinking of offering $1.2 million."

More silence. Then, "No. I am not selling it."

Another abrupt end to the conversation.

I had another conversation. This time with the One who controls the real estate market in the Tenderloin. The One who holds the keys to all our hopes and dreams. The One who has given us those hopes and dreams in the first place.

"God, if You want us to get this building, You are going to have to make it happen."

A few days later, my phone rang with a number I didn't recognize. I picked up.

"Hello, Mr. Huang?"

"Yes, this is Roger."

"I am a broker representing the building on Turk Street that you had an interest in. The owner would like to sell you the building. How much do you want to offer?"

I didn't miss a beat.

"$1.2 million."

"Let me check with the owner and see if that is doable."

I couldn't help the grin that spread across my face. Here this lady had no interest in selling last week and now she is calling me and offering me the building. Only God can bring around that change of heart.

She accepted the offer.

The broker called to arrange the down payment.

"We would like you to put down $120,000."

Now, it was my turn to take a deep breath. I always know if a project is from God, then we will have what we need. But we never seem to have the money on hand for these projects. We pray. We fast. And God provides. In His way. In His time.

"We can't afford that at this time."

They came back with another suggestion.

"What about 3 percent?"

I paused. "No, I am afraid we can't do that."

I could sense the tension building on the other end of the line.

The broker said very calmly, "We would like you to put down 1 percent."

$12,000. We didn't have $120,000. We didn't have $12,000.

"That's not going to work for us."

"What is going to work for you?"

I could feel his impatience coming through in the shortness of his tone.

"We would like to put down $100 on the building for a down payment." I knew if this was a God thing, then He could make $100 down payment work.

"$100?"

I could tell the broker thought I was joking. I wasn't.

"Yes. $100."

He exploded. "There is no such thing as a $100 down payment!"

And then he hung up on me, which is expected. What I had suggested was crazy. He knew it was crazy. I knew it was crazy. But I have known God to do things even crazier. He has shown me again and again that His timetable is not ours. His banking system is not ours. And nothing is impossible with Him. Nothing. Not even offering a $100 deposit on a million dollar building.

Years ago, I would have waited anxiously by the phone, nervous about the outcome. But I think in my long years of waiting and praying, God has taught me of His goodness. He has shown me that I don't have to worry. I don't have to be anxious. If He wants to open the door, He will. If He doesn't want it opened, then it will stay closed. And that is okay, too.

A few days later the phone rang again.

"Mr. Huang?"

"Yes?"

"We accept your down payment of $100 for the Turk Street building."

The feeling of joy that burst forth in my chest is one of knowing that the God I serve is bigger and more creative that I can ever fully comprehend. He surprises us with His mercy and kindness. He does more with $100 than the best investment banker could ever do. We gave the $100 and secured the property. We got the loan for the building along with a generous donor coming alongside us to invest in the building. God's building. God's timing. God's deposit. So as I stand here in the Thrift Store today, three years later, I know this is not a mistake. We were meant to be here. In this space. In this time. To intervene on behalf of the poor. To clothe bodies and uplift spirits. To bring beauty and light to this part of the Tenderloin. The Turk Street building is a miracle. Every day, when the residents walk through its door, they get to be a part of that miracle. That is real beauty.

~

A Letter of Appreciation from a Tenderloin Resident

Dear San Francisco City Impact,

I would just like to express my deepest appreciation and gratitude for San Francisco City Impact Rescue Mission. I receive really great support that helps me with my everyday needs including hygiene services, household cleaning products, and I have good access to clothing provided by the thrift store. Everything that this mission does for me, I absolutely need and appreciate so much.

I particularly appreciate the free medical services offered here as it is the main way for me to access healthcare. I also really enjoy the personal interactions that I have with the staff and volunteers here at the Rescue Mission. They are friendly, and I have personally witnessed the changing and supportive service that the Rescue Mission has had on my friend, Keith, which is an inspiration to me.

~

Chapter 9

A Trust Adventure

When I walk into the SFCI Thrift Store, I don't just see racks of clothes. These aren't just secondhand couches that line the walls. Those aren't just donated flowers in a bucket of water. They are concrete ways we offer hope. God cares about us in a million different ways. He is specific in the way that He ministers to each one of us. He knows our hearts and needs before they are even on our lips. His care isn't just for the people that live in the Tenderloin. That is for our staff and our volunteers, too. Sometimes it can be easy to forget that our staff sacrifice every day to serve here. They know the meaning of fasting and praying for provision not just for the people who live here but for themselves. There are no large salaries or bonus packages when you decide to work for City Impact. People do not work here because of the pay scale. They come because God has intervened in their lives and they want to intervene on behalf of others.

For many years, we prayed in payroll. Sometimes there was no payroll. Our staff members have struggled for years with finding affordable housing in San Francisco and being able to afford the expense of living in the Bay Area. The cost of gas and groceries have skyrocketed here. But we pray for open doors and believe God for provision. Even now as our finances have grown steadier, we know that He alone is the One who provides for all our needs. Many have left lucrative careers in business to join us in our work. It is amazing to see the caliber of people who have joined hearts and hands with us these past few years. It is amazing to see how God has met their needs once they have come to us.

When Pushpa was manager of the Thrift Store, she often saw her own needs and wants met in very specific ways. It isn't often that you have a biomedical engineer manage a thrift store. God has a sense of humor, and He delights in surprising us with weird jobs and new paths that we never thought we would take. When Pushpa first started working at the Thrift Store, she was searching for place to stay. She was living with friends and had just run out of toothpaste. That morning when she walked into work, she discovered a huge donation of toothpaste had been made to the ministry. In the smallest details, it seems that God is looking out for us and providing.

Before she started working for us, she loved shopping at Banana Republic. Nonprofit work doesn't usually lend itself to shopping in name-brand stores. Pushpa thought having clothes from her favorite store would be one of her sacrifices to join us, since their things were now a little out of her price range. But they weren't out of God's price range. It just so happened that someone kept donating clothes in her size from Banana Republic. God seems to care about us individually. He knows the desires of our hearts, even the ones that we don't know we have. He knew that Pushpa needed a physical reminder of His extravagance to help her remember that He was taking care of every need in her life.

In moments of doubt when Pushpa wondered if City Impact was where God wanted her to be or if she should pursue another job in her field, He kept showing up. When Pushpa was laid off from her job in the biotech industry, she began regularly volunteering at the health clinic. She thought she was just biding her time until she found a "real" job. When she had to move and couldn't find a place to live, He kept opening doors and reminding her that He was the One taking care of her. She could trust Him—all the way down to the clothes she was wearing. Following God is a trust adventure.

Pushpa's California adventure of stepping out in faith and trusting God began a few years ago. She has always been close to her family and was following in their footsteps by getting a degree linked to medicine. Several of her family members are doctors. After finishing college in St. Louis with her engineering degree, she relocated to Minneapolis, taking a job she had been offered at a new biotech startup. She worked there for six years, loving every minute of it. She loved the close-knit company and friendships that she formed there. She loved the excitement of launching new devices. Her skills caught the attention of a company in California when she came out to visit some girlfriends. On a whim, she agreed to interview with them. The company offered her a new job in research and development on the spot. She decided to take the leap. In less than a month, she had uprooted herself from her comfortable home and was driving across the country to her new life.

Not knowing anyone in Sunnyvale where she had recently moved, Pushpa decided to visit an Indian congregation in Livermore that her mom had recommended. Her first Sunday at the church, a woman came up to her and said, "Are you Pushpa?"

She was completely caught off guard. "Yes, how did you know that?"

The woman laughed and told her that she had a cousin in Minnesota who knew Pushpa and who had told her that she was moving out to California.

Pushpa had to laugh. Even though the congregation met in Livermore, an hour from her new home, they began inviting her to be with them and checking in on her. She was drawn into the family atmosphere and quickly found herself being included in the ministries in the church.

Her first exposure to City Impact was when a friend from the church invited her to attend our City Impact Conference. She loved the ways we reached out to the community, shutting down the streets and setting up ministry tents with food, backpacks full of school supplies, free haircuts, and medical advice. When her church asked her to be part of planning their own community outreach conference for the youth from several Indian churches in the area, she decided to use our conference as a model. The church had never done anything like that before, but they partnered with the Livermore Homeless Shelter and set up stations at their church, offering hats, gloves, and scarves to the residents; hosting a sit-down dinner, and including a hair cutting tent. They enlisted one hundred college-age students to serve at the stations, ministering to the poor. It was amazing.

Pushpa felt good about all that she had done to be part of the conference. Her parents had always taught her that everything good in life comes from God, and it is important to give back to Him and to honor Him with her time and money. The pastor who spoke at the conference gave Pushpa something else to think about. During his message, he talked about tithing. He said, "It's important to tithe your money to God. But what about tithing your life?"

Pushpa remembers thinking, "What? That's a crazy concept. If I turn thirty and tithe my life, then that would be three years." The thought was planted in her mind. She told God, "If you want me for three years, I can do that. I don't feel called. I'm happy with my job. I've got this career but if You call me, I'll go." She wondered, "What would it look like to give three years to God?"

At the same time Pushpa had been gearing up for her church conference, work at her company was almost grinding to a halt. She was used to being busy in her old company, helping launch a new product every six months. Her new company was slow. Too slow. She would arrive at work and there would be nothing for her to do after she checked in with her boss. What Pushpa didn't realize was that her company had decided not to pursue launching another product. Her life was about to be turned upside down.

Pushpa left for Christmas and traveled to India with her family. Her first day back to work, her boss asked her to meet with her for lunch. The clinical trials weren't going well. There was no more money for research and development. She was laid off. Her boss seemed astonished that she took it so well. Pushpa laughed and said, "You're not going to believe this, but while I was in India I was thinking about nonprofit work."

Pushpa's boss looked at her like she was crazy.

But Pushpa had already e-mailed Alex, our volunteer coordinator, after she had helped with her church's outreach. She had offered to come up and do some volunteering when her work schedule allowed. It seemed like her work schedule had just opened up. She called him and asked him when they could meet. Alex said, "Come on in tomorrow."

Pushpa thought she would be a good fit for the clinic due to her medical device background. Each day we asked her to come back. She began taking in patient information, setting up for the doctor's, and putting together hygiene kits. She left feeling exhausted. Her whole body ached at the end of the day. But she couldn't wait to come back. She was still job hunting, but she began to feel like the work she was doing with us was making a difference. She loved it. We asked her to organize all the supplies for Compassion Weekend when we do a neighborhood outreach. She put together a spreadsheet and jumped in. Alex Areces, the director of the clinic, asked her to join their evening meetings with the doctors. Her excitement about the clinic began to spill over in her conversations, and she began telling all her friends about it.

Pushpa still hadn't found a job, but we had found one for her. Christian met with her and asked her if she would want to head up our new ministry, TL Made, a social enterprise that featured work by Tenderloin artists.

She said, "Really? Are you crazy? I'm an engineer. I can't draw a stick figure to save my life."

Christian laughed and said, "You don't need to come up with arts and crafts. You just need to manage people."

"I'm still looking for jobs in my field."

He said, "We still want you."

She found out a few days later that Christian also wanted her to manage SFCI's other social enterprise, the Thrift Shop. We like to keep people on their toes. From engineer to volunteer to store manager. Not the usual career path that Pushpa would have chosen. But, once again, Pushpa took the leap, believing that God was leading her on this adventure. Life in the Tenderloin can be crazy. Life in the ministry can be crazy. Connect the two, and you get even crazier. But the craziest part of all is that God orchestrated Pushpa's journey every step of the way. When Pushpa told God that she would give her life to Him, He took her up on her offer. Her excellent management of both social enterprises led to her being our Operations Manager and School Administrator. She brings joy when she walks into a room, and a sense of organization and care to every project she touches. She is committed to loving the staff and students. That care shows in her listening ear and in everything she does.

As Pushpa takes care of the staff and operations at City Impact, as she takes care of school needs and invests her heart and talent in City Impact, God keeps showing her how He is taking care of her. She says, "I feel like my faith has become a lot stronger, and I do rely on God for everything." From housing to clothing to new opportunities to grow and learn, God is leading Pushpa on a trust adventure. He is using her in a hundred different ways. She is giving her life to Him, and, in turn, we are blessed.

~

Pushpa's Story

*T*he thrift store underwent a huge remodel at the end of April 2015, *New paint, new layout, new clothes, new floor. All the work was funded by a local church and done by staff and volunteers. Some days, the only hours we weren't at the store were between 2 a.m. and 6 a.m., so that we could sleep. The whole remodel was completed in a week and was hugely successful. Sales went up, customers were happy, all was well with the world. Except for one thing.*

I started getting restless. I felt like I could be doing more. I was very candid with my boss, Matt, our Operations Manager. He oversaw all the Department Managers at City Impact. I told him that I didn't feel like leaving City Impact but my life had to be more than replacing clothes on a hanger. I still vividly remember him saying, "Why do you always feel like you need to be doing something? He said, "You should wait on God."

I had no idea what that meant in practical terms. At the time, we had a prayer tent set up on the roof of the Jones Street building for a 24-hour prayer chain for the upcoming conference. My time slot was Thursdays from 6 a.m. to 9 a.m. I decided to implement Matt's advice the only way I knew how. I literally sat on the roof and did nothing. I told God, "I know You have a plan for me. I don't know what it is. Can You make it clear?" I didn't pray. I didn't read my Bible. I didn't journal. I simply sat there and watched the sunrise for about three hours and then went to work.

At 4 p.m. that same Thursday, I received a call from Christian saying that he wanted to talk to me Friday morning about a proposal. He said it was all good and I shouldn't be worried. I was flying home to Chicago to visit my family, so we arranged a time for a phone call.

When Christian called, he told me that Matt was leaving City Impact. He wanted me to take over as Director of Operations. I was shocked that they would consider me for such a position. I asked to discuss this decision with my family over the weekend. Less than 24 hours after I had decided to wait on God, He answered my prayer in a way that I never would have expected. I felt very unqualified for the position and felt like I was getting in over my head. I had flashbacks of when Christian first asked me to be Thrift Store Manager. I was very resistant and said I didn't have experience. I felt like Moses when he was asked to lead God's people and came up with every excuse possible.

I knew Operations would be much more demanding of my time and I would see less of my family and Indian church community. After returning from Chicago, I discussed the decision at length with Matt on the roof of Jones Street building while Christian waited impatiently for my decision. I finally asked Matt, "Do you think I should take this job?"

His response was another question, "Do you think this is a job God wants you to take?"

I said, "Yes."

Then Matt said, "Then it doesn't matter what anyone else thinks."

One of the concerns I had about taking the job was that I felt like I would lose touch with the Tenderloin community. I had begun to make friendships and was afraid that I would be stuck in an office. Matt reminded me that I could have a much greater impact in the community by supporting the department managers and being a listening ear, so they in turn could manage their staff to reach the Tenderloin. It made sense and was reassuring because that is the same way Jesus originally invested in His disciples to ultimately spread the gospel to the world.

I remember texting Maite that I had really big shoes to fill and didn't even know the full extent of Matt's responsibilities. She immediately texted back, encouraging me. I had the month of June as a transition period and officially began work as Operations Manager in July. Alex Areces, the Health and Wellness Center Director, told me that when I first came to the clinic, he entered my name in his phone as

"Pushpa Volunteer." After two years, he realized that it had never been changed and asked me if he should change it since I was now his boss. I told him to leave it that way so I didn't forget my roots.

I thought the learning curve for becoming a thrift store manager was harder than any engineering work I had previously done. Taking over Operations and Facilities was exponentially harder. It was not a 9-to-5 job, but my work as Thrift/TL Made Manager was definitely training grounds for this new phase in life. Facilities somehow encompassed more time than I could have ever imagined with a revolving door of elevator failures, roof leaks, electrical outages, maintenance requests, parking concerns, and contractors coming. I was the point person for every problem and most of the staff complaints. But I was totally thriving and had a newfound appreciation for the years of work by the Huang family. It truly is a full-time job just to keep the City Impact doors open and the lights on every day.

Along with Operations, Matt was also the San Francisco City Academy Administrator. He has continued to be a board member since leaving, but I was voted in as the new administrator. At the time, SFCA received similar attention as all the other departments. I met with each manager once a week and tried to keep a schedule similar to Matt's to maintain a smooth transition. During my ninety-day review, the primary goal was to achieve accreditation from the Association of Christian Schools International. The school had taken the summer off to regroup and focus on accreditation work, but all of this was foreign to me as I had no background in academics. By the time we entered the fourth quarter, I was finally getting into a rhythm. Then the pace seemed to skyrocket with two banquets and four holiday outreaches. The City Impact roller coaster ride kept getting faster and faster.

By the end of the school year, I realized that SFCA needed a lot more time and attention than I was currently devoting in terms of preparing for accreditation. I also started to feel like I was a jack of all trades and master of none. I didn't think any area was really moving forward. Everything was simply being maintained. In January, my office moved from Taylor to the second floor of Jones into a separate office inside the seventh- and eighth-grade classroom. By physically being present in

97

the school, my eyes were opened to so many unspoken needs of the SFCA staff. I saw that small changes could make a significant difference in the lives of teachers and staff who often were isolated to their classrooms or school office. The school soon became the bulk of my responsibilities, so I talked to Christian about officially changing my role.

My emphasis on facilities needs was replaced with challenges like being out of paper and toner, finding substitute teachers, and dealing with boys who constantly flooded the bathroom sinks, causing the fire alarms to go off. In all this, I found joy again by being able to see the cycles of poverty and addiction being broken through Jesus and education. It was helpful to know that SFCA was definitely on the right path. There was a lot of low-hanging fruit that we could grab to make quick improvements. All the board members were a constant source of encouragement, and I couldn't have done it without their help. God truly equipped me with everything I needed, just as God equipped Moses with Aaron and a staff.

The accreditation walk-through took place on Friday, March 25, and the three-day visit is planned for mid-October. This is a huge milestone in the history of SFCA and is a true testament to all those who have paved the way before me. Accreditation builds credibility for all stakeholders and will really help the school grow to the next level. My role at SFCI seems to change every six months to a year. I never could have imagined such a journey when I first started volunteering in the clinic in January 2014, but God is faithful and I continue to trust that He is still in the process of molding and refining me. I am so fortunate and thankful for God to choose me to play such an integral part in the miracles taking place in the lives of our students!

~

Chapter 10

A Building Miracle

The restaurant where I am having lunch is crowded. The door swings open as a couple comes inside. A hum of conversation fills the small space. The tables are shoved close together to accommodate as many customers as possible. The scent of cilantro and simmering chicken broth fill the air. This is my favorite place to come in our neighborhood to grab a bowl of pho, the delicious Vietnamese noodle soup that has grown so popular recently. With a little chili and hoisin sauce, it is perfect. When pastors come to visit and talk about our work, I bring them here. They get good food and a good taste of what our neighborhood is like. I push back from the table and stand up, tucking my tip underneath my plate. This is not a fancy place, but the food is always delicious and served quickly.

I catch the owner's eye across the room and wave, "Thank you so much!" He smiles and waves back, as he leans in to take the order of the couple who just came in. I have always liked getting out into the community. I know quite a few of the shop owners and the restauranteurs around our neighborhood. It is good to connect daily with the people we are trying to serve, to know them and their stories. There is not one person here in this community who does not have a story to tell. The bell on the door clangs as I step out into the bright afternoon. We always try to be good neighbors to the business owners in the Tenderloin. So many of us are trying to make this section of the city a better place to live.

One of our neighbors went through a tragedy five years ago. Their historic family restaurant on Taylor Street, open since 1937, burned down. It was just a few blocks from the Rescue Mission. Earlier, I had approached the owner, asking about renting his hotel located on Taylor. Even though it hadn't worked out, the owner was a kind man. I liked him. I felt badly about what had happened to his family restaurant. I never like to see anyone suffer. It's hard to see your dreams die. I know what that feels like. The man owned the entire block of buildings, but the restaurant sat empty after it burned. That was all about to change.

Michelle came into my office one morning two years ago. The October fog cast a dark shadow through my office window, but her bright smile always lights up my day.

"Hey, Dad! Check this out!" She handed me a beautiful glossy postcard.

I felt the weight of it in my hand. It was a real estate flyer with an architectural rendering of what this block could look like. Turning it over, I read the back. It said that the block with the historic restaurant was up for sale. There were three buildings in the parcel: 120 Taylor, 136 Taylor, and 144 Taylor. I turned the postcard over and shook my head.

"I don't know, Michelle."

"Why not? It's perfect." Michelle knew we were bursting at the seams. With the school growing, we needed the full second floor of the Jones building for classrooms. It was our dream coming true. But it was also a problem. We needed more office space and housing for our School of Ministry. We needed space. A lot of space. It was a good and bad problem to have. Good because growth is good. Bad because real estate in San Francisco is so expensive. There was a downturn in the market at the time, so it was a buyer's market. But we didn't have anywhere near the price that the flyer was asking for. Actually, we didn't have any of what the flyer was asking for.

"Dad, at least think about it."

I tossed the card onto the desk along with another pile of mail. I smiled at my persistent daughter.

"Okay, Michelle. I'll think about it."

Growing always brings growing pains. I know this, but it doesn't make it any easier. It just reminds me one more time that it is all in God's hands. If He wants us to grow, we grow. If He wants us to move, we move. If He wants us to have a new building, we will have a new building. The Taylor Street parcel was more than a long shot. But long shots are what God does best. After a few days of praying and Michelle bugging me, I picked up the phone and called the owner.

"Hey, Jack, it's Roger Huang from City Impact."

"Hey, Roger. How are you doing?"

"Great. Hey, Jack, we received your real estate flier and see that you are selling your Taylor Street parcel."

"Yes. It's a hard thing but we think it's time. We are hoping to open the restaurant somewhere else in the City. We've had several offers on it already."

My heart dropped a little.

"Well…" I took a deep breath. "We would like to place a bid on the building."

"You would?"

"Yes. Would that be okay?"

"Yes, of course."

With his blessing, we placed a bid with his broker. He told me later he didn't think I had the money. He was right. I didn't have a penny of it, but I called his broker and made the offer. In our years of ministry, there have been several moments when Maite and I will look at each other and think, "How is this happening? Can this even be real?" We had one of those moments when the broker called us and told us that we had outbid all of the other developers and that the building was ours. It was a miracle. We couldn't believe it, partly because we didn't have any money in the bank to pay for it, but mostly because God had pulled out all the stops again. There was no reason why we should have been able to outbid the other offers. I have learned that God moves us forward a step at a time. Step one was winning the bidding war. Step two would be securing the loan. Sometimes God has to perform one miracle so that He can build off of it and surprise us with an even bigger miracle.

Miracle number two came while Christian and I were sitting in a boardroom in the Northwest. We were meeting with the group who had given us a loan for the Turk Street building. They had taken a chance on us then. We were hoping they would take another chance on us, but this was a much larger loan and a much bigger risk on their part. They were a ministry-based bank that funded hundreds of ministry projects and loans around the world. They were also a financially solvent business. They make wise, careful business decisions and take their responsibilities very seriously. We are not a money-making enterprise. We are not a huge ministry with a gigantic donation base. We give out more than we bring in. This isn't a good thing when it comes to banking, but it is exactly the situation that God likes to use to show off His creativity, His goodness, and His mercy.

The building where we met was immaculate with beautiful decor. Chris and I walked up the stairs to the second floor into a pristine boardroom with a large table surrounded by chairs. I ran my fingers through my hair and took a couple of deep breaths. I knew one thing as we sat down around the glossy wood table. If this was going to happen, it was going to be God making it happen. Chris and I were just there to bear witness to it. We had nothing to offer, and we were asking for everything in exchange. We were coming to these men in good faith with a dream God had placed in our hearts, nothing more.

The president of the bank, William, came into the room along with two of his partners. "Hi, Christian, Roger. It is great to have you here today." He greeted us both with a handshake.

Christian said, "Thank you so much for meeting with us." He was as nervous as I was. They held our future in their hands.

"Why don't you tell us a little bit about this project that you want the loan for?"

Christian began to share the miracle that had come about with us winning the bid on this pivotal piece of land. He did an amazing job of telling them how our ministry was growing and the vision that we had for the Taylor Street parcel. For thirty minutes, Chris shared our heart and passion for the people of the Tenderloin.

And then it was silent.

Chris shot a look at me. I looked back at him.

No one said anything. William pressed his palms down on the table and looked at me and Chris. He drew in a deep breath and began to speak. He chose his words carefully.

"Sixty years ago when I was a young boy, I lived in San Francisco. I would take the bus across town to go pick up my mom from work so that we could go home together. My mom worked at 25 Taylor Street."

A pin could have dropped in that room. My heart was pounding in my chest. That was one block away from the parcel of buildings that we were trying to buy.

"I know that area. I know the Tenderloin. I know that neighborhood. We will fund your loan. The work you are doing is needed, and we want to help you keep that work."

Christian and I stared at each other in disbelief. This well-dressed gentleman who was the president of this large bank knew our neighborhood. How was that even possible? Was this for real? He knew the street blocks that we walked each day. He had walked them himself. He knew the great need of the people we served. And he was on our side. More to the point, God was on our side. He was pulling out all the stops. God orchestrated a beautiful symphony of events, and we were honored to be a part of it.

William is a man of great conviction and despite his powerful position, very humble. We felt that humility that morning. We felt the power of all of these men placing the interests of the residents of the Tenderloin before their own interests. We felt the hand of God guiding our steps and hearts in sync with these amazing servants. Because of their generosity and their belief that God's work was their work, we were witnessing a miracle. We were stunned, and we were grateful. Four months after Michelle handed me that glossy postcard with a picture of the Taylor Street parcel on it, we owned it. God had brought about a miracle that launched us into our next phase of ministry. This was a phase that would require even more miracles and we were ready.

~

Rebecca's Story

*M*y great grandmother's name was Anna Chuning Hsiao. She led a
pretty extraordinary life that paved the way for my family to walk
in the way of the Lord. She was born in a little town in Missouri. When
she reached the age of twenty-eight, she decided to set sail for China and
respond to God's call to do ministry overseas. She opened a missionary
station with an underground church in Beijing and began the next fifty-
four years of her life. Anna eventually married a Chinese officer, Paul
Hsiao, and had two daughters and a son, and two grandchildren (one
of them being my mom). Because she married a national of China,
the congressional statute at that time revoked her U.S. citizenship and
she was registered as a woman without a country for more than forty
years. During those fifty-four years of her life, she continued steadfastly
in her calling to spread the gospel anywhere and everywhere she went, no
matter what the cost.

It wasn't until President Richard Nixon visited China that
my great grandmother was allowed to redeem her U.S. citizenship and
return to the United States. She was eighty-two years old. She turned
one hundred years old the year I was born, in 1991, and I had the
great privilege to share this earth with her right before she passed. Anna
Hsiao left a lasting legacy for my family to always pursue the gospel at
all costs. Because of her dedication to God's mission, I believe I have
a great example to follow with everything I do. Although my life will
look different in terms of which endeavors I take, the core remains
constant. She's taught me that our time on this earth is short. If my
great grandma can simply uproot herself and spend fifty-four years of her
life in a completely foreign country in order to build His kingdom, no
task for His kingdom is too great. Her heart for lost souls and the gospel
overpowered any earthly barrier, and she was willing to look different

during her time here on this earth with hopes of spending eternity with Him. With this kind of family legacy, I hope not only to reflect the same heart as my great grandmother but to build His kingdom. I leverage all I have in my life for the lost souls in the Tenderloin district.

Recently, I caught up with my friends from high school. The high school we attended was Whitney High School in Cerritos, California, and, at the time, it was rated the number one high school in the United States. It's been seven years, and they have already created their own business, are working in some top-notch law firm, or are working their way up the political ladder. When it came to what I did, it didn't sound at all impressive—working in the Tenderloin district as the Development Coordinator at an inner city church.

A friend said, "You went to the top high school in the nation to end up working in the inner city?"

I responded with so much joy and fulfillment because I knew, for me, it wasn't about the title or what my pay was. This job brought me fulfillment. I wasn't working up any corporate ladder, but I was living to serve others. Not everyone is called to work in the inner city, but I was called to attend the top high school in the nation to end up in a successful career serving the homeless and children with everything I have. That's what I call redefining success and allowing God to work and provide.

~

Chapter 11

The Taylor Street Breakthrough

City Impact is new to Taylor Street. We have occupied space on Jones Street and Eddy for so long that they feel like home. But God is opening up new paths in the Tenderloin for us, literally and figuratively. As I walk down Turk Street toward our new building, I see some familiar faces. One of our residents makes his way up the other side of the street toward the Rescue Mission. The smells of tar and exhaust fill the air as he passes by the city workers repairing part of the road. A police officer directs traffic around the cluster of machines smoothing out the patched road.

I see some new faces too. The group of young men walking up the street together looks more like Ivy Leaguers than Tenderloin residents. They probably work at one of the new tech companies on this block. Down the street, another building is under construction. The building is being resurfaced and its "guts" are being brought out in chunks of worn out plaster and brick. Lots of work is going on in this area right now. Several tech companies have moved into the neighborhood after receiving incentives from the City to move their businesses into this small district.

Turning left on Taylor, I see the front of our building. It is a beautiful sight to behold. Like these new businesses going in, our building is stunning with new paint and bright windows. After a year of renovations, the Taylor Street building is fully operational. I push open the gate to our small parking lot. We have our own parking lot in San Francisco. That is unheard of. Most of us working at City Impact pay $10 to $15 a day to cover our parking costs. More than one of us has forgotten to refresh a street meter and come out to find a healthy parking fine. This is life in the city. Getting a dozen free parking spaces is like gold.

A team of ministry students are setting up a stage and sound equipment in the parking lot for an outdoor worship service. "Hey, guys!" I lift my hand.

They wave back, shouting, "Hey, Pastor Roger!"

These School of Ministry students bring energy to us. That energy is encouraging and uplifting. Their passion for working with the poor revitalizes us every day. Later this afternoon, this parking lot will be packed with staff, ministry students, and residents shouting praises to God in an outdoor worship service.

I open the door on the ground floor of the building. I still have to get used to stepping inside and seeing the amazing renovations that have been done here. It is an awesome sight. We have only been in this building for a year. Our main offices and leadership program have moved into the top two floors.

The exposed brick on the ground floor wall is the perfect background for the teams that come to work with us. The pitted red-and-white brick is a reminder of the city outside these walls. Outreach planning and team meetings take place in this large open room. I pass by the new elevator to take the narrow winding stairs upstairs. The state-of-the-art surroundings still overwhelm me. Every window, every fixture points back to the generous creativity of the God we serve. There is not one corner of this building that isn't being used. The administrative heart of City Impact is pumping away in this building with Chris's office and the operations staff.

Further up the stairs, you will find dorms for our School of Ministry students, complete with multiple kitchens and restrooms. I still can't believe it when I walk through this building. How good God is. How faithful.

Chris and I are getting together to talk. I kept my office in the Jones Street building when operations moved over here. We don't see each other as often as we used to. This building is a hive, at work, building and working together, to intervene on behalf of this community. Most of what Maite and I have experienced here in the Tenderloin has come in stages. Most of the miracles that God has given us, whether it is a building, a ministry or a life changed, has taken a lot of work and years of prayer to see them come into their full capacity. I think God keeps reminding us that He is in charge. We have to depend on Him completely for each project. He keeps us humble and on our knees. That is when we see His greatest creativity at work.

The Taylor Street building is a testament to God's ingenuity and His thoughtful planning. When I look back on that meeting in Oregon with the bank, how could we possibly know that William would have a connection with the Tenderloin? How could we know that his heart would be moved, and he would make this dream God placed on our hearts a possibility? In the same way, God began working in the heart of my friend Eric long before he headed up the renovation for our Taylor Street building.

Years before Eric ever stepped onto our new property, his teenage daughter took BART into the city from the East Bay. She came to the Tenderloin and worked in the Rescue Mission. Her heart was moved to help those who needed it. We couldn't know all those years ago that we would be linked together by this young woman's love for the poor. We couldn't know that years later Eric would walk out the miracle of renovating the Taylor Street building with us. But God is like that. He lays out pieces to the puzzle, fitting them together in a way that only He can.

I have always said that God doesn't just do miracles. He uses people and does miracles through them. He invites us to be a part of what He is doing. We can either take Him up on His offer or walk away. Once we have experienced one of His miracles in our lives, we think He will act in the same manner the next time an urgent need arrives. We look for formulas to try and figure out how and when He is going to act on our behalf. We shouldn't bother. He never does it the same way twice. He rarely uses the same people in exactly the same way. He doesn't want us boxing Him in with our ideas of how He should work. He is always bigger, always more amazing in how He answers our prayers than we can imagine He could be. Sometimes the groundwork that takes place before a miracle occurs is years in the making.

I don't see a problem and know how God is going to work. I just know that He is faithful and He keeps showing up. When problems come, I don't have divine revelations about how God going to solve them. My job is to pray and believe that He will solve

108

them in His own way and in His own time. I have been asked how I know what doors are going to open. I don't. I just keep knocking on doors. Some open. Some don't. But if I don't knock, they will never open.

God doesn't usually let me in on how He is going to move. I have to keep trusting Him even when I don't know how things will work out. You never know where He will take you next. You just keep following. This is what my friend Eric did.

Eric's journey was different from my own. Eric's mom and dad were seventeen and eighteen years old when they got married. They didn't have much, but they wanted their son to have the best chance at a good life so they put him in private school. Eric attended Catholic school from elementary through high school. This strict schooling gave him a strong foundation of discipline but left him feeling disconnected from God. His wife, Lori, grew up on a farm outside of Milwaukee. She had a Lutheran heritage but mostly felt that religion was about rules. Neither of them felt a strong sense of connection to God. When they met after college and fell in love, they decided from the outset that they wanted their marriage to be Christ-centered. They began the early years of their marriage by learning how to follow and love Jesus.

This decision set Eric, and his family, on his own unique journey of chasing God. Eric had graduated college with an engineering degree and began working in the tech industry in the late eighties. As the industry boomed, so did Eric's career. He worked for EA Sports and Philipps. His jobs in the operation side of things took him from New York to Europe to Hong Kong and back again. After years of endless travel for work, Eric was considering another position in San Diego. Lori wanted a place to call home where their two kids could blossom and flourish. Instead of taking on the job San Diego, Eric and Lori took off on their biggest adventure so far. They settled in Castro Valley on the ranch they had purchased for retirement.

This was a new season in their lives. A season of digging in and planting roots. They began to build up a new business in the golden hills of the East Bay, running a dog kennel for boarding and caring for animals. They didn't know a thing about building a kennel. They had owned a dog, but they didn't know much about animal care. They had never done anything like that before. But Eric wasn't afraid of taking risks. Eric had always been a hard worker, willing to put everything that he had into his job. God blessed their business, bringing them trustworthy employees and helping them build solid relationships in their community. They began attending Valley Christian Center, a growing church in the Tri-Valley Area. Their kids were flourishing. Their business was growing and expanding. Their relationship with the Lord continued to grow and deepen over the years.

Eric had always felt the pull to give back to his community and to the areas close to where they lived. When other people wanted to go overseas on missions trips, he felt like the best way to honor God was to help those around him. He wanted to invest in the needs of the ministries and nonprofits that were doing amazing work right where he lived. When his church was stalled out in the process of building its new sanctuary, Eric offered to finish the job. He and Lori had built homes and buildings for their business but had never done anything of that magnitude before. Even though he was out of his depth, Eric was moved by the need of his spiritual community. Along with his business partner and a group of loyal employees, Eric took on the project, believing they could do it.

God seems to move us forward in phases. Asking us to step out and trust Him. He invites us to do what we have never done before—believe that He will connect the dots in His time. Eric's church supports City Impact. Eric's daughter had served with us. Dots were being connected that I wasn't even aware of. I was amazed by the work that Eric and his team had done. He had completed a beautiful new sanctuary and was in the process of finishing a state-of-the-art science building for his church.

So I asked Eric about our renovating our Taylor Street building. Building in the heart of San Francisco is a completely different animal than building in the rolling hills of the East Bay. But he didn't hesitate. He wasn't daunted. With a gracious heart, he jumped in feet first. He told me later, he thought, "How hard can it be?"

Renovating buildings is an exercise in patience, especially in the city. Eric didn't realize the roadblocks that he would come up

110

against at City Hall. Or all the trips he would have to make to San Francisco. There were moments when he felt as if he was hitting his head against the wall, trying to figure out how to navigate all the permits that were required. Roadblocks were thrown up every step of the way. Money has a way of running out or just not being there in the first place. But in those places of frustration and worry, Eric kept moving forward and pushing through. I told him, "We will just keep praying." It is hard to just keep praying when bills are mounting. Eric and Lori were investing more time and money than they ever had before.

At the same time, Eric began to see God work in ways that he never had before. When the windows were delivered for the building, he didn't have the funds to pay for them and he told the window supplier upfront. The window supplier just looked at Eric and said, "We'll do it anyway." Neither Eric nor I knew that the window supplier was a believer whose church had worked with City Impact in the past. When it came time to put in the elevator, Eric didn't know how we would pay for installation, but a good friend of his stepped in and installed it. Each of the men on his crew saw God work in miraculous ways as they stepped out in faith and built the building. With each victory, there seemed to be another insurmountable roadblock ahead. With each prayer that was answered, another impossible need came up.

Getting all the permits for the building was holding the project hostage. We were at a crucial point in the construction. It can take months or even years to have permits approved in San Francisco. Setbacks are inevitable. We couldn't move forward without the proper paperwork in place. I told Eric, "We are going to keep praying." I set up a meeting with one of our supporters and chief intercessors who is also a good friend. My friend had pull with the City and was going to see if he could help us. The morning of our meeting, Eric was back at the City Planning Department, seeing if he could make some headway. I didn't know it then, but Eric had decided that if he couldn't get the permits he needed then he was going to tell me he was not the man for the job. He was so discouraged.

We had planned that he would meet my friend and me for lunch. He walked into the City Planning Department, took a number, and settled in for a long wait. The man sitting next to him asked, "What do you need help with?"

Eric showed him the paperwork and said, "I'm just trying to get this done." He showed the man the drawings and permits he needed. He was six months to two years away from getting the approval he needed to build.

The man looked at Eric and said, "I can do that for you."

Eric was stunned.

The man directed Eric to a different floor, saying, "I want you to take these drawings to that floor, and talk to this person."

Eric followed his directions and spent the next five hours working with this person in the planning building.

Meanwhile, I kept texting Eric, saying, "Where are you?" "This is an important meeting!" "This guy can really help us!" "Hurry down here." I couldn't figure out what was taking so long.

By the time Eric arrived for lunch, every single permit that we needed was in place. He never saw the man who helped him again. When Eric told us what happened, all we could do was laugh and praise God. He had come through again. Here I had set up a meeting with someone who had pull with the City and God had set up the ultimate meeting. We were all floored.

I told Eric, "Sometimes God has to make the mountain so steep than when we finally get to the top, we know it could only be Him." Our building was completed in six months. This is an unheard of time frame to build in San Francisco. It is a God time frame.

Eric said, "This is His building. When I see the building, I love the building, but I see all the stories that took place while building—my relationships with the suppliers and the elevator friend and the window guy and all my guys who work for me. I see their walks of faith and I'm just amazed! This is just so cool!" Breakthroughs come in all different shapes and sizes. As that building grew, our faith grew. God is so good to let us be a part of the miracles He is doing. Eric will tell you that when we step out in trust, we get to see the world in a whole new light. The light of God's amazing provision and generosity.

112

I walk through the building toward the glassed-in conference room. The light from the newly framed windows pours in and fills the open space. We are getting ready to pray again today. We never know how God will move next. We just know that whatever it is, we want to be a part of it.

~

A Letter of Gratitude

Dear Social Services Center,

The work that you do in the Tenderloin is truly a representation of the light of Jesus. Ever since I started coming to City Impact, I have been provided with many resources and options for personal growth. The staff and volunteers were efficient, kind, and helpful in giving me the information that I needed.

Due to your perseverance, I was able to get my I.D. through the D.M.V. at a lower cost. I appreciate this because I am currently homeless and in need of support. I am thankful for the kind words, encouragement, and counseling that I received during the process and am going to come back to this organization for any future needs.

The San Francisco Rescue Mission has been such a blessing to me, and I can truly see Jesus' work being done in my life. When I enter through your doors, I feel a sense of peace and comfort that can only be found through the movement of the Holy Spirit. Once again, thank you so much for the love and support you have given me in my time on need.

~

Chapter 12

A Beautiful Journey

San Francisco is one of the most beautiful cities in the world as far as I am concerned. Settled on the tip of a narrow peninsula, this hilly city is surrounded on all sides by the crashing waves of the Pacific and the choppy green waters of San Francisco Bay. From the top of Coit Tower perched on one of its highest hills, you can catch a breathtaking view of the Golden Gate Bridge, the new Bay Bridge, and the golden hills of Sausalito. The vastness of the Pacific Ocean is amazing. I used to take my morning runs along the Great Highway following the natural curve of the beach. The crash of the waves and the sound of seagulls diving for their breakfast were the soundtrack to my run. God's creation is always awe-inspiring.

The beauty of San Francisco doesn't stop with the beach. Tourists come to San Francisco in droves. They have a lot of beauty to choose from. They can bike the length of the Golden Gate Bridge on a cool foggy morning or catch one of the tour boats out to the Rock and see what life was like in the prison on Alcatraz. If they like historic surroundings, they can venture into the Presidio, the old army base turned National Park, and spend their visit surrounded by the lush greenness of cypress trees and the sharp scent of eucalyptus. If visitors happen come during spring, the Japanese Tea Garden in Golden Gate Park is awash with the pink and white blooms of the cherry trees. They won't find a lovelier place in the city.

But finding their way around the city to see all the sites and take in the surrounding beauty? That is a different story. Navigating the streets of San Francisco is a little like navigating a maze. It is easy to become disoriented. Tourists trying to find their way to Chinatown for a quick lunch can end up in North Beach eating Italian. Trying to get from Pier 39 to the San Francisco Zoo is a crosstown adventure. We have known more than one person to turn down a one-way street by accident and head into oncoming traffic. There are on ramps that don't seem to have off ramps. When they lose their way, they see the seamier and more desperate parts of our beautiful city by accident. There are thousands of ways to get lost in this city. Most of the tourists who end up lost in our part of town don't want to stay. They want the quickest way out.

We don't have a whole lot of sightseeing opportunities in the Tenderloin. The people who live here on these streets and in these buildings have a different view of San Francisco. Most of them never planned on living here. Most of them don't have a way to leave. While we don't have a lot of tourists in the Tenderloin, we do have some fantastic volunteers. We have people who are willing to give up hours and days to help those who are hurting. Most of our volunteers are just regular people who have problems and struggles just like you and me. They come here to join hands and hearts with us because they love Jesus and want to love the poor. Many come from beyond San Francisco.

My friend Terry drives up from Southern California regularly to volunteer. He first came for one of our City Impact conferences and had his eyes opened to the plight of our community. It happened at a turning point in his life. The son of Taiwanese immigrants, he came to the United States when he was eight years old. He came to know the Lord in high school after being introduced to a youth group by a friend. His youth pastors poured themselves into his life. Terry became a model Christian man. He married a beautiful Christian girl. Even though his early years in the States were a difficult adjustment, life now was good for him. He lived comfortably with his family in the suburbs.

But all was not well with Terry. He felt a void. Church on Sundays began to feel more like a chore. Although both he and his wife had spent years serving in church, they were both going through a crisis of faith. There had to be more to Christianity than just living a moral life. Terry was challenged by a speaker at a church he visited. The speaker asked, "What are Christians known for?" Are Christians known only for being judgmental and hypocritical? Terry didn't want that for his life. He wanted to do more and be more. He wanted to be like Jesus.

116

Terry read *Crazy Love* by Francis Chan and was challenged even more. He wanted to live his life in service. He wanted in on where God was moving. When he found out that Francis had moved to the Bay Area and would be speaking at our City Impact conference, he was intrigued. When he discovered our conference was more about service in the community than an actual church service, he decided to attend. Terry drove up from Orange County a few days early and offered to help us with whatever we needed to do in getting ready for the conference.

I was working in the kitchen when Christian brought Terry in to meet me. We connected over our Taiwanese roots. Whatever we needed that weekend, Terry was there to lend a hand. Terry left that weekend changed. God had inspired him. For the rest of that year, whenever we had an outreach Terry drove up to help. And he didn't stop there. Terry went home and started volunteering in his local soup kitchen. He is a man who loves God and loves the least of these. It is exciting when we connect with people who are moved by the same things we are. Terry's journey to San Francisco led him here, and we are thankful he keeps coming back.

A lot of our volunteers are overwhelmed the first time they come to help out in the Tenderloin. When they deliver meals to one of the buildings for the first time, the sights and smells are overwhelming. The poverty and despair they encounter can be shocking. For some of those volunteers, it is too much. They can't take it in. They get depressed and leave feeling discouraged. A few are not overwhelmed. Terry was energized by being able to dive in and help with needs that were so apparent.

My friend Matt is another volunteer who was touched when he visited us for the first time. His journey to the Tenderloin is just as unique as Terry's but he connected with our residents on a different level. Matt is one of those volunteers who came and stayed. He ran our Adopt-A-Building program for a season. The darkness of the buildings and the brokenness of the people he met there broke his heart, but not because he was overwhelmed or unaccustomed to poverty. It broke his heart because he knew that darkness himself. He knew what it was like to sit in a dark, flea-infested room, high and desperate, wondering if there was any way out. Looking at him now and hearing how Matt was brought up, you would never believe it. You would think that Matt would have easily found God and His straight path. Matt is now Assistant Camp Director at a Christian camp on the East Coast, and one of our current board members. You would never suspect that he experienced the harsh realities of life in the ways he did. But life has a way of taking detours. Matt's journey of following Jesus has been anything but a straight path.

Matt was raised in a Christian home in Florida. His dad worked for a Christian curriculum company that was part of a Bible college. He knew all about God. It seemed to him that God was a God of discipline. The more he learned about God, the more he felt judged. God had a lot of rules. Being the type of kid who questions everything, he didn't love rules. As a kid, he loved figuring out how things worked, so he wanted to know the "why" of each rule. "Why do we have to memorize so many Scriptures at school?" "Why do we have to follow a dress code?" When he questioned the rules, he could never get the answers that he was looking for. The answer "Because we said so" never sat well with him. He wanted to figure out life and how he fit into it. By the time he was in college, Matt wasn't sure God was a good fit for him.

After his sophomore year, he decided to quit school and find a job. He found his passion. It was working and problem-solving. He had always been a hard worker, and when his good friend invited him to come work at Chick-fil-A as a General Manager, he jumped at the chance. He threw himself into his work. They both had a strong work ethic and they worked well together. They energized the restaurant and got noticed by corporate headquarters. Matt loved the ethics behind the company and found the opportunity to advance. When his friend went on to launch another restaurant, Matt worked at corporate and headed up one of the restaurants in a nearby mall. When his friend got tagged to open a large restaurant in Orlando, Matt joined him. It should have been a dream come true—starting something new, working with a close friend. But something confusing was happening in Matt's life. The passion that had infused his work began to fade. It wasn't enough to hold him or his interest any longer.

Matt was recruited by Macy's in Orlando and left Chick-fil-A. The Vice President of Macy's invited Matt to be the manager at the Merritt Island store. It seemed like the perfect opportunity

118

for a new career path. They put him on the fast track for leadership in the company. But the excitement of a new opportunity didn't last. After working on Black Friday, the day after Thanksgiving, Matt knew the job wasn't for him. The path that he thought would bring him happiness didn't. The job that he thought would be a perfect fit wasn't. Matt was confused. His life wasn't turning out the way he thought it would.

With no direction, he decided to explore life in a different way. He was tired of following rules. He was tired of feeling judged. He wanted to find out what life was all about without outside influences.

Just like he had thrown himself into work, he threw himself into exploring life in a new way. Life for Matt is all or nothing. He quit his job. He became atheistic in his views. He moved back to his hometown in Florida. Instead of a chasing a career, he took odd jobs doing landscaping and bouncing at local night clubs. Matt began drinking and doing a lot of drugs. He lived without any pressures and without anyone telling him what to do or how to live. He was done with rules.

But his life began to unravel. What Matt didn't recognize was that instead of setting himself free of rules, he was setting himself up to self-destruct. He moved into a house with a bunch of sketchy neighbors. He thought he was shutting out the outside influences, but he was really opening himself up to dark, spiritual influences. One housemate, who was a Buddhist, invited Matt to read the Tibetan Book of the Dead. Even though Matt declared himself an atheist, he decided to investigate other religions. He began to read about the life of Buddha. The darkness of his life overwhelmed him. He quit doing odd jobs and became a recluse. He wrote twisted poetry and took hits of acid. He cursed God and embraced the dark. The young man who had a passion for problem-solving found himself cut off from reality.

It all came to a head one night. He was high, lying in the darkness of his hot bedroom, reading the Book of the Dead with a flashlight. He was flea bit and sweaty. Thoughts about death raced through his head. In that literally hellish moment, Matt says, "A voice came to me. It said, 'Take a look around, and turn off the flashlight.' Just like that, I realized how far I had run. I felt like I was in a cave. I knew it was God's voice. I knew there was a light somewhere up there, but I couldn't see it I was so far in that cave. That's how dark it was."

"The voice said, 'Take a look around and see what truth is.' I looked at my neighbors. I looked at the influences. Just the week before, I had written a poem cursing God. Then I turned around. He was just right there. I didn't have to turn around all the way. He was already there. That was where I experienced mercy and love and grace. It broke me. Everything became so clear to me. At that moment, I realized what I needed to do. It was above my logic. It was a moment of transformation that I'll never forget. Everything changed about me."

God met Matt in the dark. Even in his hatred of God, God still loved Matt. He chased him down and met him with His love and mercy. In that moment, Matt's breakthrough came. He found himself covered in grace, not judgment. That changed everything. His dreams. His desires. His passion. He began to read the Bible in light of God's amazing love. He began to understand that God wasn't a God of rules but a God of compassion. In the ugliest place in Matt's life, God showed up with His beautiful all-encompassing love. Matt began a new journey of chasing God back. But it wasn't in a straight line.

Over the next few years, God used his family, his friends, and his desire to follow Jesus in re-shaping him. Always with mercy. Always with love. One of Matt's friends gave him a new job at Chick-fil-A. He got involved with a community of believers and worked with a homeless ministry at the church he attended. He worked his way up through the ranks of Chick-fil-A again. When he left there after four years, he went and helped another restaurant company streamline their hiring processes. But he was still chasing God. It wasn't about rules or success or finding himself. It was about loving God and listening for His direction. He felt like God was his personal professor, teaching him about His love and grace.

God is always creative about moving us to our next phase in lives. Matt's friend was going on a mission trip to Africa. When the trip was canceled, his friend decided to come to City Impact for a week. He invited Matt to come along. Matt had no idea what City Impact was but he was always one for a good adventure. When he

120

set foot in the Tenderloin, he felt his heart breaking for the residents. When he visited the buildings, he saw the darkness. He saw the hopelessness. He saw the despair. It didn't put him off. He knew what God can do in the dark. He knew how God had set him free. Within months, Matt had quit his job, proposed to his girlfriend, and moved to San Francisco. He and his beautiful new wife, Hayley, spent their honeymoon driving from the East Coast to California. It is an adventurous way to start a marriage. But, then again, when you follow Jesus, His path is never in a straight line.

God has a funny way of getting us from point A to point B. His path always seems to involve backtracking and detours. Terry's journey led him from Taiwan to Los Angeles to us and back again to impact his own community with God's love and grace. Matt's journey mirrors a winding ride through the streets of San Francisco. God used the darkest moments in Matt's life to reveal His deep love for him. He used the memory of those same dark moments to break Matt's heart for the lost and bring him across the country to us. He used Matt's natural talents of organization and problem-solving when he worked with us in our Adopt-A-Building program. His insight and wisdom about day-to-day operations and managing staff helped us grow and change at just the right time. God's time. Matt was pivotal as Operations Manager, organizing our growing departments and putting systems into place that we still use today. We are thankful that we were a part of Matt's journey with God.

Even though God has led Matt and Hayley back to the East Coast, we can see the goodness of all that He accomplished in bringing them to us. We can't often make sense of God's path or His timing at the time, but in retrospect, we can often see its beauty unfold. There is loveliness to the winding path of God's handiwork and creativity in moving people in and out of our lives. As we work together, as we pray together, as we lean into each other, we see and feel beauty in the hearts that are healed along the way.

We may not have a lot of tourist sites in the Tenderloin. We may not have lush gardens or ocean views, but, little by little, darkness is giving way to light. And, one by one, lives are being changed. In this journey of chasing God and seeing breakthroughs, nothing is more beautiful than that.

~

Terry's Story

The big thing I took away from my first City Impact Conference was this question: "What are you doing in your context, in your life?" It's great if you are going on the mission field two weeks out of the year. That's 14 days. Your year has 365 days minus those 14 days. What are you doing with the rest of your days? As much as God stirred my heart to go up to City Impact, I also knew that it was easy to go and be stirred up just like on any retreat or missions trip and then forget about it. It is easy to pack up and go home, and then that experience becomes just an event. I didn't want my faith to become an event. I needed my faith to be something that stirs me up and sustains me.

I intentionally told the guys up in San Francisco after the conference that I was coming right back. I came back for every outreach that winter. Then, coming back home, I knew I needed to do something here. My wife and I sat and prayed after repeated trips. It was great that we were up in San Francisco with friends and in a ministry that God obviously was involved in, but what could we do here in Orange County? What about the brokenness around us?

So I took everything I learned at City Impact—the grace banquets and the outreaches of showing people grace—and went to a local soup kitchen called Mary's Kitchen. I asked Gloria, who runs it and if I could bring volunteers to bless the guests. We have been doing that monthly ever since. We have built some good friendships. We have been able to walk through life with some folks. Some have passed away in the last few years. We have been able to love on them without judging, while hoping that they find that Jesus is the best way and the only way.

I also serve on the Board of Directors now at City Impact. Three years ago, when Roger approached me and asked for my resume, I asked him, "For what?"

122

He said, "Terry, We're putting a board together and I want your resume so we can pray over it and see if you would be a part of us."

I literally looked around to see if maybe he was calling another Terry. I am not successful as far as having my own business or having wealth. I do care deeply for people. Those who are inside the church, those who are outside the church, those who are successful, those who are struggling, I know that God wants each of us deeply. I think that is what Roger saw in me. I told Roger, "I don't think I'm qualified."

He told me, "You love God. You love us. And you love the poor. Those are the only three things that I require." Looking at those three things, I guess I did qualify.

I have been on the Board of Directors now for three years. Getting to see the new building, the transition to Christian as leader and how he rallies people together has been exciting. It's been a blessing to me to be a part of this. God is doing a lot of things, and I am just happy to be a part of it. City Impact isn't just a place. It's an idea. It's God's idea. It's God's heartbeat. I am bringing that idea with me down to Orange County. It is getting people in the pews involved in what God cares about. And that is people. As for City Impact? I am looking forward to being a part of everything every step of the way.

~

An Internship Story

As told by Matthew Wong, SFCI ministry student

just want to express my gratitude toward City Impact's Life and Development Center, and more specifically its coordinator Dino Powe. I owe my current job and much of my knowledge about social work to my internship with the Life and Development Center and what I learned from Dino. Studying in college, I obtained a great deal of book learning and intellectual knowledge. Not until my experiences at City Impact did I truly get exposed to the real world conditions of poverty and homelessness in San Francisco. Under Dino's mentorship, I slowly grew more and more confident working with clients and learning how to provide counseling for them. From merely watching his interactions, I learned a great deal about how to calm people down and make them feel more comfortable.

The thing I admired most about Dino was not his people skills or his dedication to his clients, but the way in which he walked with God. Although at times drained and stressed, Dino always made time to come to the Lord in prayer and say His praises. More important than teaching me how to work with people, Dino taught me how to stay motivated by constantly reminding myself that everything I do, I do for the glory of the Lord. Because of the nature of the work, it is easy to grow weary and depressed from all the pain and suffering one is exposed to. But working with Dino proved that God can provide a person more than enough strength and joy to impact people's lives, despite these conditions. Overall, he was an excellent supervisor and role-model for me. I hope I can be the same one day to someone else.

~

A Rescue Mission Breakthrough
As told by Pastor Ralph Gella, SFCI staff member

*L*aura, the kindergarten teacher in our school, was leading an outreach. *She and her team were visiting the Aranda Hotel, delivering hot meals. Laura knocked on one of the doors. Alone in his room, Charles opened the door. Laura handed him a meal, an invitation to the Rescue Mission and prayed with Charles.*

Charles was from Texas. He had served in the U.S. Marines and worked all his life. He moved to San Francisco to be closer to his mother. While Charles was working as a security guard, he got injured and ended up on disability. He was now living in a single room at the Aranda Hotel in the Tenderloin. He struggled with alcoholism and loneliness. Most of Charles' friends just wanted to use him for money and alcohol. His drinking got worse and worse. He was lonely and depressed. With no job, no real friends and no purpose, life was hard.

Charles remembered the encounter with Laura. He had kept the invitation card pinned to his wall. He decided to go to the Rescue Mission. Charles walked into one of the services, heard the gospel, and got a good meal. He continued to come to the mission and met some good people. He also started coming to church on Sundays. Charles encountered God and got saved. He began to volunteer with me, doing office work and miscellaneous projects. He worked in the kitchen and helped clean the church.

Charles' heart was to work hard for Jesus and give back to the church. In this process, God restored his mind and gave him healthy relationships. He wasn't alone anymore. Charles was excited to serve and work hard. He joined our recovery home and helped with the Bible studies. He is now is a full-time volunteer at our Rescue Mission. Because someone had time to knock on his door and share the love of God with him and pray for him, Charles was not missed. He is saved and blessed. In return, he is such a blessing to City Impact and the community.

~

Chapter 13

Super Saturdays Are Super Again

Boeddeker Park is filled with kids this afternoon. The climbing structure is overrun with children scampering to beat each other to the top. A young mom is pushing her toddler on the blue swings, his legs kicking high with joy. The morning fog has burned off and sunlight bounces off the colorful mosaic sculpture at one corner of the playground. The basketball court is hosting a pickup game between some local teenagers. I stop, hand on the fence, and take it in. This corner of happiness on Jones and Eddy is a bright spot in the Tenderloin. The modern architecture of the clubhouse gives this new space a clean bright feeling. Our city did a good thing when they renovated Boeddeker a year and a half ago. There are about 4,000 children in our small community, and this is the one place that they can stretch out, run, and fall onto the green grass like every child should be able to do.

Boeddeker used to be an eyesore. More than that, it used to be a danger. It was a favorite spot for drug dealers to sell their wares. Surrounded by liquor stores, the park was the spot some residents chose to sleep off their hangovers. When we brought our City Academy kids here to have our daily physical education class, we did a playground check before we let the kids play. The sandbox was often used to hide cast-off needles. The park had a ledge surrounding the fenced in perimeter. Addicts used the ledge as a bench and the portable French restroom nearby as a place to get high. Hemmed in by overgrown trees, it was dark and unwelcoming. The park was a place to avoid. But it was the only place the Tenderloin kids had to play.

A small boy races across the grass, kicking a soccer ball, his head thrown back in laughter. There is not a better sound than the sound of children laughing. That sound of joy breaking free and filling the air is exactly the sound that should fill this park. When I did a hunger strike twelve years ago, sitting in front of City Hall, praying for God to intervene on behalf of the Tenderloin, I also, by letter, asked our City to do its part in taking care of our community. It was a desperate thirty-three days of prayer and no food before we saw any movement. Thirty-three days of cold nights sleeping on the hard flagstone in front of City Hall, of believing that God could do what we could not do.

In the way that only He can, He began to move on the hearts of City officials. It was an amazing sight to see the street sweepers begin to care for our streets, to hear of liquor licenses denied, to see a strip club next to our school close its doors not because the City ordered it, but because the owner passed away. And all these long years later, I stand here at Boeddeker Park. It is not a cleaner park. It is a brand-new park. It was totally transformed. We think our prayers end when we stop praying, but God keeps working. God keeps moving. God does more than we can ever hope or dream.

The God I chase is a big God. He likes surprising us over and over again with His goodness. We can't out dream Him. The crosswalk light by the park turns green and the traffic slows. Crossing to the corner of Jones, I can't help wondering what the years ahead hold for us. Some would say we have done enough here in the Tenderloin. Some would say we have enough programs and that we have offered enough services. Maybe we have bought enough buildings. But the truth is that what we do at City Impact has never been about programs. It has never been about buildings. It has never been about looking good to church groups or getting a better reputation in the nonprofit community. It has always been about people. The people that God loves. We want these people in our community to feel the hope of God in their own lives. We want these kids to feel that.

As I cross Eddy Street, the shouts of the kids at play still ring in my ears. I know that what God wants to do here won't be done this year or the next. It won't be done until each one of these precious children knows how much He loves them. We won't be done until they sense His presence in each and every one of their hearts.

Twenty-five years ago, our real ministry here began with kids. We launched Super Saturdays. We invited kids from the neighborhood to come play games, eat snacks, and learn about the God who loved them and would never leave them. For years, we met each Saturday and laughed together, played baseball, and sang songs. We prayed for miracles to take place in their hearts and for their lives to be made new. We loaded up as many kids as we could fit into vans and got them out of the Tenderloin to the beach and to the Blessing House in Fort Bragg. Back in those days, seatbelts were optional. We went for volume and could fit fifteen kids per van.

We wanted to open their eyes to the goodness of the world and the goodness of the One who created it. For years, we met, rain or shine, loving whatever kids showed up on Saturday. When another one of our dreams was realized with the opening of City Academy, we began to focus our attention on the kids in our school. When we brought our Super Saturday program to a close, it was because we didn't have the manpower to continue them, not that we didn't have the heart to keep reaching these neighborhood kids.

Our manpower has changed over the last decade. I am headed back to the office to meet with a few young people who have come to City Impact to work alongside us. The greatest difference in these last seven years of ministry here in the Tenderloin has been the increase in staff and ministry students. We have a lot more hands working together, dreaming together, praying for breakthroughs here. With the School of Ministry students, we find that God continues to open new doors of ministry. He opens some old ones, too. We have re-started Super Saturdays.

There is no one more precious or more in need of intervention in this corner of San Francisco than the children who play at that park. We have not relaunched Super Saturdays because we want one more program. We have relaunched Super Saturdays because Jesus loves kids. We know that not every child in the Tenderloin will be able to attend our school or come to church on Sunday, but we know parents are always looking for a safe place for their kids to learn and have fun. We want to be that place.

I am mentoring the staff workers who have relaunched Super Saturday. Starting something from scratch is never easy. You can't just open the doors and expect people to show up. There are relationships to build with parents, flyers to pass out, lessons to plan, and hours of prayer that are needed. In our get-what-you-want-when-you-want-it culture, ministry in the Tenderloin can come as a shock. Breakthroughs can be years in the making. It can take a year of Saturdays and prayers upon prayers before one child comes to know Jesus. This is what I share with these young people. You believe and you hope, you fast and you pray, you show up, but God is still the One who has to move on our behalf.

One of our young staff members, Manny, knows what this is all about. He is part of the relaunch team. He is twenty years old, but he already has lived a couple lifetimes. His own transformation didn't come overnight. He knows the importance of reaching these kids at a young age and instilling hope. One of four kids in his family, Manny comes from Los Angeles. In his neighborhood, the pull of gangs was strong. The money, the drugs, the close-knit relationships were all attractive. A lot of children join gangs when they are middle school-aged. While many join to feel safe and have a sense of protection, they are committing themselves to a life of violence. The young children set out to prove themselves to the older gang members by doing whatever is necessary. Loyalty is everything.

Manny's half-brother, who is eleven years older than he is, was a sergeant in one of the most powerful gangs in the area. He started leading a crew at age ten. By the age of twelve, he began running away and having run-ins with the law. He left home at the age of sixteen to live the gang lifestyle. Manny's mom searched the streets at night, looking for his big brother. Manny knew the suffering that his mom went through while trying to keep his brother from the gangs. But Manny loved him. He loved spending time with him. His brother bought Manny video games when he came over, and they would stay up late having fun. Manny felt safe and loved whenever he was with him.

One night, Manny was staying with his brother and cousin when he saw them going out with a couple of spray paint cans. He asked where they were going. They said, "We are going to cross out some names." He didn't realize that this task was part of his cousin's gang initiation. He tagged along. At two in the morning, they found themselves under a bridge in rival gang territory. They were going to cross out some graffiti put up by the rival gang. Manny heard a shout. Looking over his shoulder, he saw a group of teenagers running toward them. They were members of the other gang. Manny, his
130

brother, and cousin split up and took off running. But Manny's ten-year-old legs could not carry him fast enough. Within moments he was on the ground surrounded as they began to beat him. What happened was a blur. The pain was overwhelming. Manny's brother told him later that they hit him with bats. He had run back to save him.

In that beating, Manny knew the reality and brutality of gang life. Even though his brother saved him from being killed, he experienced a kind of violence that he never had felt before. But he also loved that his brother saved him. Even in this time of overwhelming pain, he was drawn to him. His mom did everything she could to keep Manny out of the gangs. He tested as gifted in school and received awards for different accomplishments. She tried to get him to focus on school, but the lure of gang life was strong.

In middle school, he began drinking and doing drugs, trying to build up his reputation. In high school, he wasn't a full-fledged member of the gang but he became a courier for them and then a dealer, moving drugs. Over the years, Manny's parents had begun attending his uncle's church regularly. Manny went to church to see his cousins on the weekends. He even began to play drums for the worship team, but his heart wasn't in it. His heart was turned toward making a name for himself. He wanted to be someone. He loved the sense of purpose that he got by supplying drugs for his friends

His parents prayed for Manny. They could see him going down the same road as his older brother. A path that led to prison. They tried to keep him away from people they thought could influence him to give in to the gang lifestyle. They transferred him to a magnet school in Compton to get him away from bad influences, but he took the bad influences with him. He began supplying his friends at the new school with weed and Ecstasy. He loved the feeling of being able to give his friends something that they needed. But his gang affiliations and dealing got him in trouble with the law. Manny was on a path toward destruction.

Manny's story could be the story of any child in the Tenderloin. The pull of money, the sense of belonging, the desire to be someone of importance, these things are what they all experience. Manny's older sister found us at City Impact and was working with us here. She invited Manny to come visit her. She wanted her brother to be safe and away from the gangs. She told Manny, "Come up and be with me and I will send you a round-trip ticket." And in the way that only God can do, He began to set a chain of events in place.

God was intervening on Manny's behalf. He knew the plan He had for Manny, and it didn't include drugs or prison or death. It included forgiveness, a new heart, and a new life. Manny just thought he was getting on the bus to visit his sister. Manny didn't know that God was answering his parents' prayers and getting him out of the gangs. He didn't realize that the Tenderloin was the door to the new path God had for him. He didn't know that his sister had bought him only a one-way ticket. He didn't know that within a few months of arriving he would enroll in our internship program. He didn't know that God would give him a dream, warning him that if he went back home he would die. He didn't know that God would change his heart one day at a time until his greatest desire was not to supply his friends with drugs but to supply the kids in the Tenderloin with the truth of who Jesus is. He didn't know that he would be one of the people relaunching Super Saturdays. He just thought he was getting on a bus. God knew that Manny's real journey was just beginning.

God knew that Manny was the perfect candidate for reaching the kids in these neighborhoods. In the miraculous way that God chases us down, God chased Manny down in the Tenderloin. He has changed his mind-set about life. He has changed his desires. And with each passing day, He is teaching him, growing him, and changing his heart. His passion has changed from building his reputation to building God's kingdom. His passion is to open these kids' eyes to the love of Jesus. It is a long way from the gangs of LA to Super Saturdays in San Francisco. But some breakthroughs require distance. When the kids from the Tenderloin show up this Saturday at 230 Jones Street to play games and hear about Jesus, Manny will be there. He has been transformed in the Tenderloin, transformed by the love of Jesus, by His mercy and His grace. Transformed, just like Boeddeker Park, just like me. As the kids jump around and sing praise songs to Jesus this Saturday, we are praying that His transforming love will open those same doors of mercy and grace for them.

~

A Super Saturday Update

As told by Bethany Gella, SFCI staff member

*D*uring our first Super Saturday of the year, we had eighteen kids, including a couple of new ones. A new mom came in with her six-year-old son and her infant baby. She found a flyer that we put near her door and decided to check it out. Right now, she is temporarily living with her mom and looking for her own place to live. She told me that her son had been pleading with her to take him out of the house, but she didn't know where to take him in the community that would be a good environment. She decided to give Super Saturday a try. Since they came a bit late, they missed the games. They arrived during worship, but her son jumped in dancing with everyone else and looked like he was having a blast. His mom later told me that he LOVED to dance and sing. She loved everything that we did and told us that she would be back next week! She also asked for information about our school, since she was interested in that as well.

~

Chapter 14

Love Comes Full Circle

The face of the Tenderloin has begun to change slowly over time. The area still has sex shops and liquor stores and ratty hotels, but new industries with new money have begun to push into the neighborhood. Dot coms and new businesses are changing the faces of some buildings. Nicer restaurants dot the corners and draw in a steady stream of young businesspeople. Boeddeker Park gives the children of the Tenderloin a safe place to play. There is a stronger police presence now with a police station located directly across the street from 230 Jones Street. The city has stepped up street maintenance. The street sweepers come through on a more regular basis. These are good things. Positive shifts. People always respond well to beauty.

But in a lot of ways, the needs of the Tenderloin remain the same. Tucked up inside the crowded apartment buildings are people who long to be free. Free from drugs. Free from loneliness. Free from the oppression of poverty. Out on the street corners, there are still kids looking for a way out, selling drugs and joining gangs. People still find their way into the dark corners of the neighborhood to pay for sex and companionship. Then there are the hungry. Little children who still go to bed with their stomachs cramping. As new business moves in, the cost of living has increased. Rents are rising, even for tiny studio apartments. Those living on Social Security wonder how they will make it month to month. Families struggle. There doesn't seem to be much relief. In that way, the Tenderloin has stayed the same.

That is why we are here. We long to intervene on behalf of the poor. We want to put food in bellies and hope in hearts. We can't do it all. But we can do something. With the help of our volunteers, we are doing more for more people than we ever have before. This

134

is the heart of Christ at work in us and through us. Some of our volunteers come to City Impact, thinking that we have all the answers or that we have figured out the secret to following Jesus. If they stay long enough, they find out that what we have figured out—that we are as broken as the people we serve. Each one of us has had struggles. Each of us has personal weaknesses and heartaches we have to endure. Only the constant love of Jesus has made the difference in our lives. We may look different from the people that we serve, but our hearts are the same. It is the hope of Jesus at work in us that keeps us reaching out. We recognize ourselves in the faces on the street. We want those faces to know the same love we have known.

We are not so removed from the people who live from meal to meal and depend on the kindness of others. I remember the days when I was a homeless runaway teenager. At seventeen, I escaped my abusive dad by sleeping in Golden Gate Park and in the lobbies of the surrounding apartment buildings. For two years, I knew what it felt like for the wind sweeping in off the bay to cut through my thin clothes and for hunger to clutch at my stomach. I knew the despair of trying to figure out where my next night would be spent and the loneliness of not having a close friend. The struggle is real.

I was able to find a way out of that life by working my way up through the hotel industry. But the fear of it, of not being able to take care of myself, of not having work or the security of a home? That stuck with me for years. It is what fueled my relentless obsession to succeed. When I began to serve the poor, I couldn't look at a father with his young kids without thinking, "That could be me." Or into the vacant eyes of a young drug addict without thinking, "This could be my daughter."

When I look into the eyes of Laura, our kindergarten teacher at City Academy, I feel as if I am looking into the eyes of my adopted daughter. We got to know Laura when she was just in her teens. She grew up on the streets and in the alleyways of the Tenderloin. The daughter of Cambodian refugees, she knows the ins and outs of this neighborhood better than I do. There is nothing about homelessness, hunger, abuse, loneliness, and fear that I can teach her. Seeing prostitution, drug abuse, alcoholism and gang life were just a normal part of her childhood. She never knew any different.

She has known it all. The death of her mother left her older brothers alone, trying to take care of her on the streets. When Laura gave her heart to the Lord at age sixteen, she began a long journey of breakthroughs that were beautiful to behold. Laura is a beautiful woman inside and out. For the last fourteen years, we have watched her grow and blossom, becoming more than she ever thought that she could become.

Laura began a two-year internship with us when she was eighteen. She came to us when our ministry was small and when our main workers were just Maite and me and our kids. Maybe that is why she feels like one of my daughters. We have learned together and grown together and loved each other like family. As the ministry has grown, she has grown with it. During her internship, Laura was required to work in all different areas of the ministry, in the Rescue Mission, in the office with me and Maite, and in the school. Laura found that her gifts led her toward teaching.

She was working as an aid in the kindergarten class when the kindergarten teacher left. She stepped into the role of kindergarten teacher and never looked back. Her natural ability to work with kids shines through. She is has a unique way of connecting with the small children that walk through her door. She understands their struggles and their needs. She has lived in their shoes and in the apartments where they reside. She has known fear and hope and scarcity like they have. And she has a heart for them. Laura loves the kids that live in the Tenderloin. She wants them to live a different life than she did.

When I think about the slow changes that have taken place in the Tenderloin, it seems similar to the way God works in lives of the residents. You don't see a lot of overnight changes. You don't see drastic shifts in behavior. Over time, when people have yielded their lives to the Lord, you see the building of character. You see hearts continually turning toward the light instead of the dark. And you see love happen in big and small ways.

When Josh began working with our internship program a few years ago, Laura didn't see anything more in him other than a fellow team member. She saw him on Sundays at church and at different events but wasn't attracted to him. When he began helping out in the classroom, she noticed how well he worked with the

136

children and how kind he was toward them. Laura says that because Josh was young and handsome and a passionate hard worker, a lot of other girls liked him. She didn't consider liking him because he was seven years younger than she was. She tried to set him up with girls his age, but he wasn't interested.

Laura and Josh worked side-by-side teaching and then started leading a Bible study in one of the buildings with a group of residents. They saw each other's good and bad sides, their strengths and struggles. Laura slowly began to realize that she liked Josh more than a coworker. And Josh felt the same way about her. He asked Laura to be his girlfriend one night after Bible study. When she said yes, their entire world shifted. Laura never thought she would find someone who fit with her, who would love her, and would be as passionate about ministry and the kids of the Tenderloin as she was. But after three months of dating, Josh did more than surprise Laura. He surprised all of us.

During a session at our City Impact Conference, in front of a crowd of 2,000 people in the historic Warfield Theater, Josh dropped to one knee and asked Laura to marry him. She couldn't believe it. When she said yes, the cheering was so loud it sounded like a rock concert. Laura was excited and scared all at the same time. She remembers telling God, "I didn't think I would ever get married. That I would find someone to love me."

I remember having those some feelings when I found Maite. I remember being utterly surprised that someone would want to be with me for the rest of her life. There is something healing about another person telling you that they love you. Marriage isn't an easy road. But it is a good road when you are on it with a person who loves you and loves Jesus. You show up every day. It is a commitment. Sometimes it is exciting and fulfilling. Sometimes it is difficult and frustrating. But the love that flows between two people in marriage can be the most powerful, beautiful relationship in life.

Seeing Laura's transformation from bride to mother has been another joy for us to watch as well. Love multiplies when a baby shows up. Baby Kolaiah is a beautiful round-cheeked one-year-old little girl now. Her face lights up with joy around her mom and dad. She is loved by her parents and by every person at City Impact. Becoming Kolaiah's mom has radically changed the way that Laura sees God's love and how He treats her. She says, "When I look at her or am frustrated or nervous for her, I look at how God is with me. How He's so patient with me and cares for me."

Laura marvels at how much her life has changed over the past fourteen years. She went from living on the streets to becoming a wife and a mom, from trying to get high to escape the pain of life to ministering daily to children and helping them know the love of Jesus. Love has come full circle. Laura says, "I never thought I would be at the place I am at now. Married, having a kid, being a teacher. I never thought I could ever be those things, but by God's grace, I have fallen more in love with Him and with people."

God seems to do that. When we let Him, He transforms us. When we chase Him, He embraces us. When we ask for His help, He invites us to be a part of the solution. Laura didn't know what she was getting into when she asked Jesus into her heart and gave her heart to God over a decade ago. But He knew His plans for her. To love her. To shape her. To give her a family. To grow her into a kind, loving teacher who teaches children about the love of Jesus every day. About the love that has so radically changed the course of her life.

Laura, Josh, and Kolaiah live in the Turk Street building. They live in the Tenderloin but they are not living there with hopelessness. They are living there with a purpose. Love has come full circle for Laura.

As I walk to my car to head home, a cool fog drifts in from the bay. I know life has come full circle for me, too. Maite and I are ready. Ready for whatever God has for us next. Ready for the next person to connect with. Ready for the next breakthrough. We know it is coming because that is what God does. He continues to break through every day with His hope. With His love. With His promises. He is letting us be a part of it. And we are grateful.

~

Conclusion

A New Path

Walking on the beach near our home is one of Maite's and my favorite things to do. Standing next to her now, with the breeze coming off of the waves, her hand clasped in mine, I can't believe how far we have come. Being near the enormity of the Pacific, the crash of the waves and the scent of the salt air has always been a balm to my spirit. In my most stressful times, in moments of prayer and fasting for the future of our ministry or for our kids, the thunder and roll of the waves were a constant. They are a reminder of the greatness and vastness of the God who chases after us and loves us.

We have been contemplating our next phase of life and what it will bring us. More challenges, I am sure. More joy. More hardship. This is a given in this city. More time to fast and pray. And more breakthroughs. God is so good to us.

As the salty waves roll up on the shore, surging toward our feet, one after the other, they sing of the everlasting faithfulness of God. He keeps moving forward. He keeps building. He keeps transforming lives. Like wave upon wave. His mercy is unceasing. His love is deep and wide and long. His purposes and promises build one upon the other, crashing down over us, soaking us with His peace and grace. When we look at all He has accomplished in us and in our ministry in the last thirty years, we are overwhelmed. We remember our crude beginnings, our sleepless nights and countless disappointments. What has been accomplished has been accomplished by the hand of God alone. He is the One who deserves all the glory and honor for each miracle that has come about. He is the One who receives all the attention. Whatever joy, whatever hope has poured into our corner of the Tenderloin is due to Him and His amazing presence. He is extravagant in His love for us. And Maite and me? We are just along for the ride.

People think that we are successful. That after all this time, we have it all figured out. It is easy to get caught up in the idea that we have done the hard work to get us where we are. That our sacrifice, our time, our energy has enabled God to do this work we have devoted our lives to doing. But that would be a lie. God is the One who accomplishes the work. He is the only One who is still accomplishing the work in lives and hearts and minds. He is so generous that He lets us get in on what He is doing. It is by His faithfulness and His faithfulness alone that City Impact has grown and that Maite and I and our kids have been changed. It is because of His faithfulness and love that each person in the Tenderloin who has experienced a breakthrough has been transformed.

Success isn't about having money. Success isn't about having a big ministry. Success isn't attracting big names to your events. Or speaking at big churches or selling lots of books. Success in God's eyes doesn't really look like what we think it does. Real success in this life is chasing God. Real success is having Him let us in on the good things He is doing. Real success is experiencing His breakthroughs in our hearts and in our attitudes and in our outlook in life. Real success is realizing that He is changing us from the inside out for the better. Real success is loving Him and letting Him always have the spotlight in our life.

Our culture, even our faith culture, tells us that success means wealth and fame. That we should chase after performance and search for endless new ideas. It urges us to seek after those who are successful. Intimacy with God seems less important than meeting those who are powerful. We think that by being with others who are successful we might become a better person or we might succeed. We chase after building our own business in the name of God. We spend a good amount of our time looking for ways to pull important people into our circle. But we are never satisfied. There is never enough. Loving this world and all its glamour is meaningless. It will disappear like the grains of sand under my and Maite's feet being swept out to sea. But spending your life chasing God and loving those around you? That is true success.

Our struggle for success in this life reminds me of the words of Solomon in Ecclesiastes 5:8–20 (NIV):

140

If you see the poor oppressed in a district, and justice and rights denied, do not be surprised at such things; for one official is eyed by a higher one, and over them both are others higher still. The increase from the land is taken by all; the king himself profits from the fields.

Whoever loves money never has enough;
whoever loves wealth is never satisfied with their income.
This too is meaningless.

As goods increase,
so do those who consume them.
And what benefit are they to the owners
except to feast their eyes on them?

The sleep of a laborer is sweet,
whether they eat little or much,
but as for the rich, their abundance
permits them no sleep.

I have seen a grievous evil under the sun:

wealth hoarded to the harm of its owners,
or wealth lost through some misfortune,
so that when they have children
there is nothing left for them to inherit.
Everyone comes naked from their mother's womb,
and as everyone comes, so they depart.
They take nothing from their toil
that they can carry in their hands.
This too is a grievous evil:

As everyone comes, so they depart,

and what do they gain,

since they toil for the wind?

All their days they eat in darkness,

with great frustration, affliction and anger.

This is what I have observed to be good: that it is appropriate for a person to eat, to drink and to find satisfaction in their toilsome labor under the sun during the few days of life God has given them—for this is their lot. Moreover, when God gives someone wealth and possessions, and the ability to enjoy them, to accept their lot and be happy in their toil—this is a gift of God. They seldom reflect on the days of their life, because God keeps them occupied with gladness of heart.

God has good work for us to do. He has breakthroughs that He wants to bring about in our lives. And He is clear about how He wants us to spend our days. Jesus, Himself, said, "Love the Lord your God with all your heart and with all your soul and with all your mind. This is the first and greatest commandment. And the second is like it: 'Love your neighbor as yourself'" (NIV). So loving God and loving your neighbor is what is most important in this life.

How are you loving God? How are you loving the people God has put in your life? This is what brings meaning to life. This is what brings about breakthroughs.

Squeezing Maite's hand, I ask her, "Are you ready for what's next?"

She laughs and says, "Let's go, Roger."

I love her laugh. It catches in the wind as we turn to walk back up the beach. This is a new path. We are taking it one step at a time, waiting for God's direction, listening for His voice. We are going to keep loving God, we are going to keep loving each other, and we are going to keep loving the people that God puts in our lives. Especially the least of these.

We want to stay focused, rooted, and faithful in all situations. We want to endure hardship and do what is asked of us. We exist to give and to serve. There is nothing better. We want to continue to see God move. We want a spiritual awakening to break out in the streets of the Tenderloin. We want it to spill into our entire city and overtake our country and our world. That only happens one person at a time. One person experiencing a breakthrough of God's love and mercy breaking through the darkness and illuminating them with the power of the Holy Spirit.

As you have read *Breaking Through*, I hope you have been inspired by the One who has rewritten each of these people's stories and who brought about the miracles in their lives. I hope you recognize that God wants to rewrite your story. He wants to do miracles in your life. I hope you will seek His will in your life. Know that you are important in God's eyes. You don't need to chase after others so you can feel accepted. Chase God. In Him, you have your destiny. You were created to do good works that He has prepared for you in advance. He has a road map for you. God wants you to break through and seek His purpose for you. Get close to God and find your life's success in loving Him and those He has brought into your life. You will never be disappointed.

May God in His mercy open up your understanding that life is short and you are to live according to His purpose. God bless you and keep you in your journey ahead.

~

Thoughts on Breakthroughs

Prayer Is Vital.

We pray for everything out of desperation. Maite and I are not articulate or flowing in our prayers, but our desperation is evident. Every need is prayed for. Through prayer, we receive permission and blessing from God. We pray for everything because He is faithful and attentive. We are always praying and hoping. It's our lifeline!

Hard Work Is Important When We Do God's Work.

When we work hard, God sees and He knows. He blesses diligence and rewards hard work in a tangible way. Often, when we are fixing a room or working on a building project, people start calling because God is sending workers and finances to help with the project.

Sacrifice Can Mean Giving Up Your Possessions.

We don't have the spiritual gift of poverty, but we do know that if we need to serve Him we better give up material things and be free of wanting. Our want list is minimal. We surrender our wish list to God so we can be completely free in His Presence.

Giving Up Our Time, Energy, Money, and Days Off Is Part of What We Do.

When we are in a ministry that requires so much of us, we just pour it all out. We are in survival mode all the time. We know every day is important, so we give our best. It's now or never. Looking back, we are glad we did it. It's rewarding, but it takes time to see the results and benefits that God has for you. In our case, we didn't see movement for almost thirty years.

Opportunity Comes Along Once in a Lifetime.

We have learned to be attentive when God is moving. Almost all the important opportunities we have had come our way have come through a simple prayer, a phone call, or a short conversation. One conversation with a lady brought a $10 million renovation for our school building. A simple phone call brought us a building worth $1.2 million. Talking with a church of 400 brought over 300 people to our Christmas outreach. A visit by three ladies for fifteen minutes brought over 3,500 people from their church in Menlo Park to help us. Every person is important. Every conversation has a purpose.

Being Selfless Is Part of God's Work.

We have to be selfless so we can see the bigger picture. When we are fully occupied with ourselves, we miss what God wants us to see. This work started because I contemplated the situation of a child being harassed. It changed my destiny. It made me a different person. I wonder at times what life would be like if I didn't care at the moment. We would have missed out on the calling on our lives.

Looking Out for Others Is Important.

We have learned that when you spend your time caring about the welfare of others, God will take care of you. People have great needs but they don't know how to ask. We want to be proactive in caring for others. Most of the time, even when we find out about people's personal needs, they still do not know how to ask for help. We want to be attentive to their needs and help them in some small way simply because God has helped us countless times. People in general are busy and they miss the important, small details like helping the sick, the broken, and the least.

Trust God for Day-to-Day Tasks.

Our work has caused us to seek God. Maite and I often do that together. It's never been easy to trust God. I didn't have the maturity or enough trust to know God can do everything. I might have heard others say God can do everything, but I hadn't experienced that. As time went by, we learned that God can be trusted. He will come through with everything we need. We trust God more and more each year. We learned to expect less and less because He knows exactly what I need. God is trustworthy.

Steer Away from the Attention that We Crave.

We have learned always to give God the spotlight and attention He deserves. We won't forget where we came from. God will never have to fight for His spot. We make sure we don't take His spot.

Spiritual Awakening Is Vital in God's Work.

If we don't have a spiritual awakening, then we have nothing. Salvation is important but salvation can't be measured. It is by faith. A spiritual awakening is noticeable. It is tangible. We see the homeless, our supporters, and our volunteers come around because they experience that personal spiritual awakening. Spiritual awakening takes place in different places and through different individuals in this line of work. When we gather together in one place, you feel their passion.

Spiritual Climate Is Important in the Territory God Has Given Us.

We shouldn't look at numbers and excitement alone. Sometimes we seek methods or look to our past experience to create that spiritual climate. Other times we look at stage presence and the person's speaking skills. Spiritual climate is about a critical mass gathering in a place. They don't need performance, stage presence, or special message to enlighten them. They are filled with joy and expectation.

146

They are changed from within, therefore the atmosphere changes. We experience that more frequently as we labor here year after year.

Movement Comes from God.

When a group of believers does not do what God asked of them, then God brings about a movement. When we came to the Tenderloin community in 1984, there were lots of movements but God planted us here without money, connections, influence, and talent. We believe God wanted a movement that was solely dependent on Him. He knew we were willing and obedient.

The Supernatural Comes from God.

The work we do is from God. We need the Spirit of God to do the work. We need the supernatural, and it only comes from the Presence of God. All we can do is ask with humility and wait for God to grant our desires. Revival comes from the Holy Spirit. Salvation comes from the Holy Spirit. He blesses us with buildings and daily provisions so we can do the work of God. It has not come from us, and it is not for us to enjoy or boast about.

Prayer Is the Key to Everything.

It always comes back to prayer. This is not because we are spiritual. We are simply desperate. Our work was not noticed until about seven years ago. For twenty-five years, we survived on God's mercy alone. We remember how we came with nothing. Every now and then, people left food at our door for our family. We remember the tough days, and it was such a struggle. We will not forget God's kindness to us and our family. God is attentive and faithful.

~

Afterword

by Christian Huang

What describes a good Christian father? By many people's standards today, I believe, my dad would have fallen short. My father never did devotionals with me. He never took me to a baseball game. We never talked sports or did hobbies together. He never talked to me about the birds and the bees. He didn't do a lot of things that many people think a good Christian father should have done. Yet, at age seventeen, I met Jesus, decided to follow Him, and was called into ministry, following in my dad's footsteps.

On the flip side, many young people who grow up in Christian homes lose their faith eventually. I didn't. Why? I think it is because the greatest gift my dad gave me was that he proved his faith in Jesus to me by his actions. He fasted, he prayed, he got himself into impossible situations. He lived his life in a way that the reality of Jesus was inarguable. He loved God above family and ministry. In hindsight, that is the greatest gift he ever gave me.

Growing up, I stumbled, fell, and disobeyed, but I could never doubt that God was real because God's hand was really active in my dad's life. Contrary to popular teaching, many times, my dad put ministry first before the family. He worked overtime. He did many things that people of balance teach against. In the end, it was worth it. It was the smartest thing he could have done, considering that eternity is real and Jesus' commands are important. It's amazing to see that as he put God's work first, God took care of his desires on the back end (Matt. 6:33). Although we aren't a perfect family, all four of his kids love Jesus and know Him personally. His faith in God and his obedience in living out the mission of God was so much better than anything my dad could have said during a father-son game or date.

Many times when talking about City Impact, I quickly share about the work we do but then focus more on the fact that City Impact is an idea. The idea is that one man or woman can make a difference! That is the story of my dad, and that is the story of many people in this book.

My dad was a Taiwanese immigrant, dropped off in San Francisco in the 1970s during the middle of the hippie movement. He didn't understand a word of English, was abused for eighteen years, and met Jesus at age twenty-seven through Jimmy Swaggart. According to the world's standard, that is not a good formula for preparing someone to do great exploits for Jesus. According to God, it'll do just fine. The fact that my dad, Roger, has been used by God only proves that one man or one woman can make a difference!

You don't have to be talented or gifted. You don't have to make perfect life decisions in a calculated way to position yourself for greatness. You only need to grab ahold of God and get busy serving others. Greatness isn't really measured in incredible action taken for God. It is usually found in just taking simple actions marinated in love. Love is the ingredient that makes almost any action great. Love is the ingredient that makes any work eternal. Gifts are temporary, love is eternal (see 1 Corinthians 13).

That's what my dad, Roger, and every person in this book have done. They've simply obeyed the commands of Jesus, served with love, and broken through. Be encouraged today as you read this book, since you too can make a difference! If you don't know where to start, book a mission trip, come tour City Impact, or join the School of Ministry. Reading other people's stories is great, but God is more interested in your story. Remember, one man or woman can make a difference!

~Christian Huang

About the Authors

Roger Huang is the founder of City Impact Ministries and the pastor of San Francisco Worship Center. He began ministering in the Tenderloin District of San Francisco thirty years ago with the help of his wife, Maite Huang. Together, they launched a food bank, City Academy elementary and junior high school, a thrift store, a rescue mission, a free clinic and community outreach programs serving thousands in response to God's call on their lives to serve the poor.

Roger immigrated to California at the age fifteen from Taiwan. Being raised in an abusive home, Roger left home at the age of seventeen. He worked his way up through the hotel industry to become a successful auditor. After his marriage to Maite, they both found the Lord through the television ministry of Jimmy Swaggart. They became highly involved in their local church. Roger led teams of men on fasting and prayer retreats. During a pivotal turn of events while in the Tenderloin, Roger felt God call him to the poorest of the poor in that area.

Roger's and Maite's lives were turned upside down as God began to lead them on a journey of service, prayer and fasting in the Tenderloin over the next 30 years. Leaving his work as an auditor, Roger went full time into ministry. God has responded with miracle after miracle as he and Maite seek God and pray over their community. Their adult children and their spouses all serve with them in their various ministries in the Tenderloin.

Susanna Foth Aughtmon is the mother of 14 year old Jack, 12 year old Will, 9 year old Addison and the wife of Scott, the lead pastor of their church plant, Pathway Church, in Redwood City, CA. Susanna has led worship, worked in children's ministry and done the odd janitorial job here and there during their ministry.

In 1994, she graduated from Bethany University, in Santa Cruz, California, with a B.A. in Social Science emphasizing Psychology and Early Childhood Education, pursuing a career working with children. She began writing full time in 2008.

She has written *All I Need is Jesus and a Good Pair of Jeans: The Tired Supergirl's Search for Grace* (Revell 2009), *My Bangs Look Good and Other Lies I Tell Myself: The Tired Supergirl's Search for Truth* (Revell 2010) and *I Blame Eve: Freedom from Perfectionism, Control Issues and the Tendency to Listen to Talking Snakes* (Revell 2012).

She has contributed to the 2013, 2014, 2015 and 2016 editions of Guideposts' *Mornings with Jesus*. She has co-written *Chasing God: One Man's Miraculous Journey in the Heart of the City* (David C. Cook 2013) with Roger Huang, *Need You Now* with Plumb (2014), *A Trip Around the Sun: Turning Your Everyday Life into the Adventure of a Lifetime* (Baker 2015) with Mark Batterson and Richard Foth, and *One Year. One Dress* (Baker 2016) with Bethany Winz.

Read Susanna's blog at www.tiredsupergirl.com

~

Acknowledgments

I thank God often for His ability to lift up the hopeless and helpless. There is a level of the supernatural that we have not been able to discover simply because we have spent so much time wandering in the wilderness. God has given me a chance to serve Him in a most wonderful way. I am privileged to serve in this inner city work. What an honor!

My glimpses into God's spiritual world have given me hope, joy, peace, and love. I see potential in everyone. I dream for them and hurt when they don't see their way out of their misery. *Breaking Through* tells the stories of people breaking through that misery as they get close to God. Suddenly, something happens. God is real, He is with us, and He wants our attention.

I want to thank Maite for being with me in this work since day one. It's been over thirty-one years and we are still together. We continue to trust God to bring forth a great spiritual awakening in this great city by the bay. Maite, I thank God often for the love you have shown me.

Michelle, thank you for being there for me. I can always come to you and seek your advice. Your love for the family is real. God will reward you for your dedication to the family and to the Tenderloin community. Thank you for writing the foreword for this book. May God bless Jody, Isla, and Hunter.

Chris, thank you for going all out for God's work in the Tenderloin community. You have done well. Your leadership is God-given. Your love is real, and you sincerely care for everyone that comes your way. Stay close to God. Thank you for writing the afterword for this book. May God bless Cori, Malachi, Mica, Maiya, and Levi.

Leslie, you have been faithful to the children in our school. Your dedication and passion for the community bring so much joy and love. You have given up your time to serve weekly. You continue to bring hundreds of people from your church each year to help and serve in this inner city work. God bless you.

Kristen, thank you for staying still and loving us. You are passionate in everything you do.

Ted and Sara Lucas, thank you for giving to and serving the City Academy. You have shown so much grace and generosity.

Eric Fabianac, you are a gift from God. You rebuilt a four-story building with limited resources. God used you to get all the permits we needed. You are a man of God with so many talents. God bless you.

Tom Dowd, thank you for being a friend to us. God bless you.

Todd and Jill Weinberg, thank you for giving to the inner city work. God bless you.

I want to show my gratitude also for the following people who contributed their time and stories to this book and to the work of love in the Tenderloin: Michael Hamada, Rebecca Hsu, Joe Bess, Ralph Gella, Dino Powe, Laura Osborn, Alex Quock, Alex Areces, Hubert Pun, Bill and Patty Moll, Kent McCormick, Alyssa Choo, Terry Lu, Manny Coronilla, Noah Blakely, Bethany Gella, Pushpa Samuel, Sarah Bomar, and Vanessa Brakey, Veasna and Elaine Chea, and Matt and Hayley Duerstock.

There are so many more contributors to the making of this awesome inner city work. We would not be able to see the success, year after year, without you. To each City Impact and City Academy staff member who works endlessly to bring the hope of Jesus to this district, may God bless you and your loved ones.

There are so many more people who gave their lives and hearts to the work at City Impact and in the Tenderloin. If I haven't mentioned your name, know that you are not forgotten by the One who loves you so much. He is so pleased with your heart of love for the poor. I am thankful for each volunteer who has walked through our doors and blessed our lives. May God bless you richly and may you experience His great love and breakthroughs in your life.

SAN FRANCISCO
CITY IMPACT
BOOK A MISSION TRIP

Short term missions is designed to equip and mobilize your church to intervene on behalf of others and take your training back home. We engage teams in the work God is doing in the inner city of San Francisco. Experience one-on-one evangelism, hands-on ministry, and come alongside long term efforts planted in the community.

DAY | OVERNIGHT | WEEKLONG
Missions Seasons
Spring + Summer (March-August)
Fall + Winter (September-February)
Come for a tour to learn more!
Email booking@sfcityimpact.com
Learn more at sfcityimpact.com/missions

(415) 292-1770 | booking@sfcityimpact.com | 136 Taylor St., San Francisco, CA 94102

SAN FRANCISCO
CITY IMPACT

We exist to intervene on behalf of the people in the inner city of San Francisco.

We are an inner city church that mobilizes people to intervene through 14+ ministries including a Rescue Mission, K-8 School, Health & Wellness Center, School of Ministry, an Adopt a Building initiative, Social Services Center, Volunteer Center and Social Enterprises.

Rescue Mission
Food bank and community dining room that serves and distributes thousands of hot meals & groceries.

City Academy
A private K-8 school offering inner city children quality education, personal tutoring, & after school programs.

Health & Wellness Center
A medical & dental clinic offering urgent care, medical specialists, community health education, & patient advocacy.

School of Ministry
Christian higher education to train leaders in theology & hands-on urban ministry. *Offers highest level of accreditation through Northwest University.

Adopt a Building
An initiative to build relationships on every floor, & every door of the Tenderloin that will lead people to life transformation.

City Impact Church
Our local church that serves & gathers as one body, on mission, experiencing God.

Social Services Center
A center that finds housing, shelter, jobs, & other needs for people in the inner city.

Volunteer Center
The department that oversees equipping & mobilizing volunteer team members to serve.

Social Enterprises
Bringing dignity & job training to the people of the inner city of San Francisco through TL Made & our Thrift Store.

City Impact Conference
A one day conference filled with worship & outreach in the inner city of San Francisco.

If we don't go, who will?
SFCITYIMPACT.COM

(415) 292-1770 | info@sfcityimpact.com | **Physical**: 136 Taylor St., San Francisco, CA 94102 | **Mailing**: PO Box 16217, San Francisco, CA 94102

SAN FRANCISCO | SCHOOL OF
CITY IMPACT | MINISTRY

The City Impact School of Ministry builds Christian leaders who intimately know God and his Word, serve people with humility and love, and fulfill the mission of Jesus in all aspects of life.

Through the School of Ministry, you will:

1 **Serve** in tangible ways to develop humility and bless others.

2 **Make disciples** through long-term relational ministry and share the Gospel.

3 **Train in the Word** and be mentored by our full time staff.

4 **Lead others** through learned training and experience.

SAN FRANCISCO
CITY IMPACT

Speaking Requests for
Roger Huang and Christian Huang

Roger Huang
Founder
San Francisco City Impact
Author of *Chasing God*
and *Breaking Through*

Christian Huang
Executive Director
San Francisco City Impact
Founder of City Impact
Conference

Hear about City Impact's work.
Be encouraged to intervene on behalf of others within your own context.

For speaking arrangements, email
development@sfcityimpact.com or learn more at
sfcityimpact.com/speakingrequest.

SAN FRANCISCO
CITY IMPACT | CHILD SPONSORSHIP

San Francisco City Impact exists to intervene on behalf of the people in the inner city of San Francisco. All of this is made possible through a monthly $38 shared sponsorship from someone like you! When you sponsor a child, not only is a sponsored child's life changed forever, but yours is as well.
Inspire a child to dream big today!

How do I sign up?

WEBSITE
sfcityimpact.com
/sponsor

PHONE
415.738.6017

EMAIL
sponsorship@
sfcityimpact.com

- You'll get a sponsorship starter kit. Then you can begin correspondence with your child!
- Watch your child grow. You can send letters, cards, photos, packages, and more, or even visit!

BEGIN SPONSORING TODAY
and receive a complimentary copy of *Chasing God*!

415) 292-1770 | sponsorship@sfcityimpact.com | 230 Jones St., San Francisco, CA 94102